THE DAO OF THE MILITARY

TRANSLATIONS FROM THE ASIAN CLASSICS

The

DAO

of the

MILITARY

Liu An's Art of War

Translated, with an Introduction, by Andrew Seth Meyer

COLUMBIA UNIVERSITY PRESS   New York

COLUMBIA UNIVERSITY PRESS
Publishers Since 1893
New York   Chichester, West Sussex
cup.columbia.edu

Copyright © 2012 Columbia University Press

Library of Congress Cataloging-in-Publication Data
Bing lüe xun. English.
   The dao of the military : Liu An's art of war / translated, with an
introduction, by Andrew Seth Meyer ; foreword by John S. Major.
     pages cm. — (Translations from the Asian classics)
   Translation previously published in: The Huainanzi. New York :
Columbia University Press, 2010.
   Includes bibliographical references and index.
   ISBN 978-0-231-15332-4 (cloth : alk. paper)
   ISBN 978-0-231-15333-1 (pbk. : alk. paper)
   ISBN 978-0-231-52688-3 (e-book)
   1. Military art and science—Early works to 1800.   2. Taoist
literature, Chinese—Early works to 1800.   I. Liu, An, 179–
122 B.C.   II. Meyer, Andrew Seth, translator, writer of added
commentary.   III. Title.
   U101.B5713 2012
   355.02—dc23

                                                                        2011047621

Cover image: Wellcome Library, London

CONTENTS

FOREWORD

W hen an ancient Chinese military theorist wrote the classic *Military Methods of Master Sun* (popularly known in English as *The Art of War*), he could have had no idea that his book would still be famous nearly twenty-five hundred years in the future, consulted as a guide to strategy not only on the battlefield but also in adversarial situations of all kinds. Master Sun's famously cryptic aphorisms, such as "When you assemble your army and formulate strategy, you must be inscrutable," have inspired thousands of participants in management seminars around the globe. Many people today who know nothing else about China know of *The Art of War*. Less widely understood is that *The Art of War* is not unique; there are a number of ancient Chinese treatises on military matters, and they are by no means all the same. What we have chosen to call *The Dao of the Military: Liu An's Art of War* is one such alternative "Art of War." It comprises "An Overview of the Military," a chapter in the *Huainanzi*, an important compendium of philosophy and political theory written under the sponsorship of Liu An, king of Huainan, and presented to the imperial throne in 139 B.C.E. As these pages will show, its view of military matters is quite different from that of *The Art of War*, and different in interesting and important ways.

The publication of the first complete English translation of the *Huainanzi* in 2010 made that encyclopedic Han-dynasty work accessible to a wide audience for the first time. The product of more than twelve years of toil by a team that included Andrew Meyer and me, along with Sarah Queen and Harold Roth, the *Huainanzi* translation invites scholarly attention on a text that has hitherto been somewhat neglected by students of early Chinese intellectual history. That statement requires some qualification. Every early China specialist for generations past has known of the *Huainanzi*. It is described in standard reference works, and many sourcebooks and anthologies of Chinese literature include at least a few passages from the text. A number of translations into English and other Western languages of single chapters or small groups of chapters have been published in recent decades, along with a few interpretive scholarly works. Nevertheless, it has generally been the case that few people have actually read substantial portions of the *Huainanzi*, certainly not in the original classical Chinese. The *Huainanzi* has been a text to dip into rather than to read extensively, a text to mine for an apt quotation or a passage parallel to one in some better-known text rather than one to read for its own intrinsic interest. The book's ancient bibliographical classification as a "miscellaneous" work, though originally not pejorative, encouraged a view of the *Huainanzi* as a mélange of quotations from earlier sources, an unoriginal compendium of relatively minor importance.

The new English translation of the *Huainanzi* radically challenges that view by taking seriously the claims made for the text by its patron and general editor, Liu An (179?–122 B.C.E.). In his poetical postface to the work (chapter 21, the final chapter of the text), Liu An makes two audacious claims for his book: first, that it so effectively synthesizes the best features of all previous books as to render those source texts superfluous, and second, that its reach is so broad and comprehensive as to make unnecessary the writing of any other works in the future. Both claims are obviously wildly overblown, but they nevertheless make clear that the *Huainanzi* was intended as a comprehensive survey, for a royal audience, of all the essential knowledge of its era. And reading the text from beginning to end makes clear that far from being a miscellaneous grab bag of quotations, the *Huainanzi* is carefully structured to embody a particular view of the cosmos, humankind's place in it, and the role of human culture and institutions in a well-ordered society. Read from that point of view, it offers a commodious and fascinating window into the intellectual life of early Han China.

As longtime students of the *Huainanzi*, we hope that the publication of our complete English translation will prove to be a valuable stimulus to the small but growing field of *Huainanzi* studies, encouraging (especially) younger scholars to explore in depth some of the many potential topics of enquiry opened up by the translation itself. *The Dao of the Military* is one of the first to take up that challenge. I am delighted that one of the members of the translation team has now taken the further step of analyzing a chapter of the *Huainanzi* in much greater detail than was possible in the brief chapter introduction in the complete translation. I hope that the next few years will see a surge of studies of particular chapters or themes in the *Huainanzi*, all of which will enrich our understanding of early Han thought.

The book you are now reading contains the text of Andrew Meyer's translation of chapter 15 of the *Huainanzi*, "An Overview of the Military," essentially unchanged (except for the insertion of additional notes) from its appearance in the complete translation volume. What is new here is Meyer's extensive analytical introduction to the chapter, which brilliantly demonstrates that (true to Liu An's vision for the *Huainanzi*) the chapter is both firmly lodged in the tradition of early Chinese military literature and approaches military matters from its own particular and extremely interesting point of view. Far from being simply a repackaging of earlier military treatises, "An Overview of the Military" is a strikingly original contribution to the genre. Meyer organizes his analysis under four rubrics that cumulatively provide a comprehensive account of the text and highlight its unique features.

The first rubric situates "An Overview of the Military" in the context of early Chinese military literature. Meyer shows that the emergence of that literature at the beginning of the Warring States period coincided with the development of large-scale infantry armies and corresponding battlefield tactics; military thinkers such as the unknown author of *The Art of War* began to explore the challenges and opportunities created by the changing nature of warfare. As Meyer demonstrates, the emerging genre of military writing was highly controversial, alarming Confucius and other masters who were committed to a social vision in which warfare was an aristocratic pursuit hemmed about by ritual restrictions. New forms of warfare aimed at political aggrandizement, territorial conquest, and the annihilation of opponents—and a literature advising rulers how to take advantage of these trends—were anathema to early China's old guard. By the time the *Huainanzi* was written, several decades into the Former Han dynasty, the raising and maintenance of large-scale conscript armies had become a routine aspect of government policy, and military writings were a flourishing and widely accepted genre of political literature. However, "An Overview of the Military" acknowledges but does not simply replicate the military literature of its time. Rather, it reorients the heritage of that literature to suit the new circumstances of a unified empire claiming to rule "all under heaven."

The role of the military in Liu An's vision of imperial government leads to Meyer's second rubric, exploring where and how "An Overview of the Military" fits into the *Huainanzi* as a whole. The entire *Huainanzi* is organized around a central metaphor of root and branches, or, as we might say today, principles and applications. The first eight chapters of the work deal with roots: sagehood, self-cultivation, the nature of space and time, and so on. The remaining twelve chapters (leaving aside chapter 21, which is a postface summarizing and integrating the whole work), in contrast, deal with branches: politics, ritual, customs, education, and the like. "An Overview of the Military" is placed as the fifteenth of the work's chapters, marking it very much as a branch— important but not fundamental. This implicitly contradicts the famous claim made in the first line of *Master Sun's Military Methods* that "warfare is the greatest affair of the state." For the *Huainanzi*, in contrast, the military is just one of many important matters that the ruler must deal with in governing his realm.

The *Huainanzi*'s ideal of an enlightened, self-cultivated ruler who wields military power only when necessary to preserve the peace of the realm, and never for aggression or conquest, was rooted not only in Liu An's philosophical beliefs but also in his political situation, as Meyer shows in the third part of his analysis. "An Overview of the Military" thus emerges as a response to specific historical circumstances. Shortly after the Han dynasty was established in 206 B.C.E., the eastern half of the empire was divided into semiautonomous kingdoms parceled out to the dynastic founder's kinsmen and loyal supporters. This arrangement would have struck many contemporaries as an entirely natural return to normality after the Qin dynasty's brief (and apparently failed) experiment with radical centralism. Liu An was an imperial kinsman and territorial king within this Han neofeudal structure, having inherited his father's title of king of Huainan. It was very much in his personal and political interests, therefore, to defend the legitimacy and privileges of the Han kingdoms against what proved to be strong and sustained pressure from the imperial center to abolish them and return their territory to central control. This explains the text's repeated use of the stock phrase that the ruler's most vital use of military force was to "sustain the perishing and revive the extinct"—that is, to defend the legitimate interests of the established aristocratic lineages. The *Huainanzi* does not argue for a return to a Zhou-style aristocratic political model; indeed, one of the central tenets of the text is the need for the ruler to adapt to changing times. But at the same time, it warns against the overreaching tendencies of the new-style bureaucratized, militarized state. Liu An's vision of empire is one in which the ruler employs military power only in defense of peace. Aggressive military action on the part of the ruler, he argues, is a threat not only to the immediate target of that violence but also to the ruler's own long-term interest in maintaining a sustainable political order.

Meyer concludes his analysis of "An Overview of the Military" by examining the relationship of that text to the doctrines of Daoism. Without venturing to address the troublesome question, what is Daoism? he shows that the text's insistence on the importance of the ruler's self-cultivation and achievement of such qualities as "spirit illumination" and "spirit transformation" (an insistence found throughout the *Huainanzi*) derives from and builds on concepts central to such foundational Daoist texts as the *Laozi* and the *Zhuangzi*. For Liu An and his circle of clients who contributed to the writing of the *Huainanzi*, self-cultivation was not to be sought or achieved primarily through study and learning, as the followers of Confucius professed; for the *Huainanzi*, erudition was a "branch" rather than a "root" pursuit. Rather it consisted of the sustained and disciplined practice of "techniques of the mind," such as particular forms of meditation and yogic exercises that emptied the mind of distractions and permitted the practitioner to achieve oneness with the ineffable Dao itself. The ideal military commander, too, through self-cultivation would achieve the ability to "see what is not seen" and to "know what is not known," so that he could be neither attacked, defeated, nor defended against. In the hands of a spiritlike commander in service to a sagelike ruler, military force could remain in effect a permanent potentiality, so filled with potency that it seldom or never would need to be employed—a Dao of the military indeed! This aspect of "An Overview of the Military" places the text, as Meyer points out, firmly in the long line of works that contributed to the development of Daoism as a religion and a system of thought.

Armed with Meyer's astute and extended analysis of the text, the reader turns to the heart of this book, the translation of "An Overview of the Military." And that is a treat, not only in seeing in translation the military doctrines expounded by the text and explored in depth by the translator but also for the beauty of the chapter's language and the literary merit of its composition. Those are aspects of the *Huainanzi* as a whole that always come as a surprise to people not closely familiar with the text: it is not only interesting for its intellectual content but admirable as literature as well. Liu An was well known as a superb literary stylist in his own time, and his influence shows on every page of the *Huainanzi*. Whatever his personal role in the composition of the text—and he probably had multiple roles as patron, editor in chief, and coauthor—he made sure that the book would be a good read. The military chapter's extensive use of parallel prose, for example, faithfully mirrored in the translation, contributes to the pure pleasure of reading the text as well as adding rhetorical heft to its arguments. Whether this translation of "An Overview of the Military" is read as part of the complete and unabridged *Huainanzi* translation or in this stand-alone version, it is an important contribution not only to the study of early Chinese military thought but to the study of Han literature as well.

In our own time, the classical military literature of early China, especially *Master Sun's Military Methods* (*The Art of War*), has come to be curiously influential. If you go to a bookstore and look for a copy of *The Art of War*, you will be most likely to find it in the business-book section. Its insightful strategies and ruthless battlefield tactics have become metaphors for the less violent, but no less contested, competition of the modern capitalist marketplace. This is not to say that its military focus has been altogether lost; Mao Zedong was a professed admirer of Sunzi, and *The Art of War* is on the assigned reading list of the U.S. Army War College. But nowadays, China's most famous ancient general is known mostly as a management guru. It is interesting, then, to think of what the impact of "An Overview of the Military" might be if this volume, too, finds its way to the business-book shelves. Where Sunzi proclaims that "warfare is the greatest affair of the state" and argues for a take-no-prisoners attitude of deceit, surprise, and intimidation, Liu An proclaims military force to be the enlightened ruler's last resort for the maintenance of peace. What will today's self-styled "masters of the universe" make of that? Perhaps one can at least hope that the text's emphasis on the ruler's (or CEO's) self-cultivation will encourage a richer and more nuanced attitude toward competition in pursuit of society's goals. "An Overview of the Military" creatively complicates our understanding of the nature and employment of military methods, whether on an ancient Chinese battlefield or in a modern-day boardroom.

John S. Major

A NOTE ON THE TRANSLATION

I translated this text as part of a full translation of the *Huainanzi*, executed by a team including John S. Major, Sarah A. Queen, Harold D. Roth, and myself, published in 2010. It is keyed to the critical text of the *Huainanzi* prepared by the Institute of Chinese Studies and edited by D. C. Lau and Chen Fong Ching. At periodic intervals, the translation is marked with the chapter/page/line of the corresponding Chinese text. Where the translation departs from the critical text, generally on the basis of some proposed emendation by a Chinese scholar, this is indicated in the notes. Proper names are romanized using the Mandarin pinyin system, with the exception of the tyrant Djou (Zhou), so as to avoid confusion with the homophonous Zhou dynasty. Several Chinese terms are left untranslated and appear in italics: *li*, *ren*, and *zhang* (traditional units of measure); *qin* and *se* (traditional musical instruments); and *qi* (a cosmological concept without a clear English equivalent). Glosses of proper names are provided at their first occurrence in the text, in notes.

Two aspects of this translation are conventions that were decided on with my cotranslators as a standard for the translation of the entire work. The text is broken into twenty-six numbered sections. Although these are not present in original editions of the *Huainanzi*, they were determined on what I perceive to be the logical structure of the text, for ease of reading and citation. Because parallel prose, especially, and verse are important components of the *Huainanzi*'s rhetorical structure, the translation presents parallel prose lines and verse as parallel lines of English, indented and set line for line.

THE DAO OF THE MILITARY

INTRODUCTION

In 139 B.C.E., Liu An (179?–122 B.C.E.),[1] king of Huainan,[2] presented a text to Emperor Wu (r. 141–87 B.C.E.) of the Han dynasty (206 B.C.E.–220 C.E.), his recently crowned cousin. It had been composed by a group of client scholars under Liu An's direction and was known by the eponym of its patron as the *Huainanzi* (*Master of Huainan*). This *Huainanzi* was unlike any text ever seen before. Divided into twenty-one sections, it covered a vast array of topics, ranging from astronomy and geography to logic and rhetoric, state organization, ritual observance, and beyond. It was not merely an almanac or encyclopedia, however. Ingeniously organized, it attempted to demonstrate how all its disparate forms of knowledge and practice could work in tandem as an organic system of dynastic rule. Indeed, it claimed to have accomplished what no text prior to that time had achieved: an integral synthesis of all the varied traditions of thought, practice, and inquiry that had arisen in the world since the dawn of civilization.[3]

The aims of Liu An's literary enterprise were wildly audacious. At basis, it was designed to be the perfect curriculum for the emperor in training, a distillation of all knowledge the monarch would need in ruling the world. Beyond this, the *Huainanzi* offered itself as an ideological blueprint for the Han dynasty as a whole. In 139 B.C.E., the Han, China's first enduring united empire, had been in power for less than seventy years. The Han had followed on a centuries-long epoch of disunion and warfare; thus its institutions and political culture were still in a state of flux.[4] The *Huainanzi* proposed to provide the Han court with a consistent and integrated worldview, one that could give shape to the dynasty's identity for itself and its subjects.

The text claimed that its structure and content were a function of cosmic necessity, that it was modeled on the fundamental order of the universe (as is discussed in the following). In fact, however, the necessity the *Huainanzi*'s authors served was somewhat less grandiose and more culturally contingent than they would have admitted. Han-era intellectuals were the legates of an elaborate and sophisticated literary culture bequeathed to them by the pre-imperial epoch of classical antiquity, especially the Warring States period (481–221 B.C.E.). In order to substantiate the *Huainanzi*'s claims of comprehensiveness and universality, its authors were compelled to demonstrate that they had accounted for all the major strains of thought and expression the classical age had produced.

As its name suggests, the Warring States was a period of unremitting conflict. Although nominally united under the suzerainty of the kings of the Zhou dynasty (1045–256 B.C.E.) for most of the era, for a period of roughly 250 years the Chinese world had in fact been divided among a few large, wealthy, militarily powerful, and mutually hostile kingdoms, all locked in a constant zero-sum contest for survival. It was an era in which policy was dominated by military concerns, and one that saw the rapid evolution of all aspects of warfare: technological, organizational, political, social, and cultural.[5] Unsurprisingly, it simultaneously saw the rise of a rich literature on military affairs, as policy makers and thinkers struggled to comprehend rapid changes on which their very lives might depend.

The most famous example of this military literature is the *Sunzi bingfa*, or *Military Methods of Master Sun* (often translated as *The Art of War of Master Sun*). The *Sunzi*, however, is only the most outstanding extant product of a very voluminous corpus. The *Wuzi*, *Weiliaozi*, *Sima fa*, *Taigong liutao*, and *Huangshigong lüe* are other surviving military texts from the era,[6] and other composite texts such as the *Lüshi chunqiu*[7] and *Guanzi*[8] contain examples of the genre. Beyond these, the bibliographical treatises of the imperial histories list many military writings that have since been lost.[9] The authors of the *Huainanzi* were thus faced with an expansive body of work that could not be ignored if their text's claims of comprehensiveness were to be at all credible. Thus as chapter 15 of the *Huainanzi*, we find "Bing lüe," or "An Overview of the Military." As its title suggests,[10] "Bing lüe" was written as a synthesis of the entire corpus of military literature inherited from the classical era; it draws on all the major existing military writings from that time and presumably includes (without citation) other material from military works now lost. Aside from bringing together all the diverse works of military letters, "Bing lüe" addresses all aspects of military affairs, from tactics and strategy to logistics, organization, political economy, cosmology, and the fundamental morality of warfare itself. The *Huainanzi* authors thus set out to produce the "last word" on military affairs, a treatise that could subsume and thereby displace all the many military writings that had preceded it.

Although the work is highly synthetic, it is not unoriginal. The *Huainanzi* authors exercised editorial discretion in selecting which aspects of the inherited military corpus to include in their work and made innovative choices in juxtaposing and integrating the material out of which they built their treatise. Moreover, the Former Han (206 B.C.E.–9 C.E.) had seen great changes from the Warring States period that had produced the classical military works; thus the *Huainanzi* authors were compelled to adapt this material for a new time and a new set of social and political conditions. What they produced, therefore, is not a wholly derivative work but an original and distinctive treatment of military affairs.

There has been one previous book-length study of "Bing lüe" in English, that of Edmund Ryden.[11] I draw on Ryden's analysis in presenting my own reading of the text, but my approach is somewhat different. As a philosopher, Ryden focused principally on the philosophical and literary dimensions of "Bing lüe," which are indeed rich and cannot be overlooked in any study. My perspective is that of an intellectual historian, however; thus I endeavor to elicit meaning from the text chiefly by situating it in the social, political, and cultural context in which it and its component parts were produced.

In the following pages, I explore four essential contexts for the historical study of "Bing lüe." The first is the long tradition of military writing of which "Bing lüe" is a part. If we are to understand both the inherited military wisdom that the *Huainanzi* conveys and the novel contributions that it makes to the tradition, we must explore the origins of the military writings and the distinctive discourse to which they gave shape. From there, I proceed to an investigation of the place of "Bing lüe" in the structure of the *Huainanzi*. Liu An and his clients had undertaken an extraordinarily elaborate and complex intellectual project, the overall construction and tenor of which inevitably inflected the discrete subtopics treated in the work as a whole. In order to fully understand the *Huainanzi*'s unique approach to military affairs, we must understand this chapter's place in the text's universal vision. Third, I read "Bing lüe" in the context of the court of Huainan and the sociopolitical position of its patron, Liu An. Finally, I examine "Bing lüe" in the context of the broad history of Daoism and discuss how it may be read as perhaps the earliest thoroughly Daoist treatment of military affairs.

The Terrain of Life and Death 生死之地: "Bing lüe" 兵略 in the Discourse of "Military Methods" from the Warring States to the Han

"The most persistent sound which reverberates through men's history is the beating of war drums."[12] Such sentiments are commonly expressed, inclining us to view military affairs as human universals lacking true cultural and historical differentiation. If such were true, we would expect all military literature to be alike. One society could not have much to say about war that differed greatly from that said by any other. The application of military force is a function of power, and because power is profoundly rooted in the universal material needs of all humans (food, clothing, shelter), we are accustomed to assuming that power operates the same way in all communities.

In fact, however, the conditions under which conflict arises and the ways in which it transpires vary greatly according to time, place, and culture. A "star war" between the kingdoms of two Mayan *ahauob* was a very different phenomenon from an engagement between two

Bronze Age Greek *poleis*. Military force requires the coordination of human efforts on ever larger scales; it thus imbues power with a cultural dimension rooted in the beliefs, attitudes, and expectations of the individuals that make up a society. This being true, fundamental changes in the way a society organizes and utilizes military force require corresponding changes in the basic beliefs, attitudes, and expectations that rule the sanctioned use of violence in that community. This dynamic is made dramatically manifest in the development of ancient Chinese military literature.

War had been occurring in China for over a millennium before the appearance of the first writings of the military corpus, despite the fact that literacy had existed for almost as long. The tradition of military letters appeared in China in response to very particular and dramatic changes occurring in Chinese society and politics, changes that were unique to the evolving historical situation of Chinese civilization. These writings thus gave shape to a discourse that bore the distinctive imprint of the Warring States period.

The epoch and society known as the Warring States emerged from the cataclysmic collapse of the Zhou dynasty. The Zhou kings had established their throne in 1045 B.C.E. with the conquest of their overlords, the Shang, setting in motion the longest dynastic reign in Chinese history. The extraordinary longevity of the Zhou throne was due largely to the initial success of their rule.[13] The Zhou kings retained centralized control over a base area in the abundant Wei River valley, enabling them to maintain military superiority within a segmented realm. Beyond the royal enclave, the Zhou established their kin and trusted allies as regional lords, responsible for maintaining local order and assisting in the defense of the Zhou throne against all threats, external or internal. These regional rulers were bound to one another and to the Zhou kings by a complex network of ceremonial exchanges, communal sacrifices, and regular intermarriages.[14]

This rule by a combination of military coercion and ritual suasion was enormously successful, so much so that the domain of the Zhou kings expanded to more than twice the size of that of their Shang predecessors. This success should not be misinterpreted as a pacific age, however. Although the Zhou were effective managers and, through their doctrine of the Mandate of Heaven, cultivated a powerful mystique around their throne, their rule was never the period of unalloyed harmony mythologized by later Chinese writers. The Zhou and their vassals were warrior-aristocrats; they were bound to demonstrate their martial valor in contests of arms. Moreover, in a world of tangled kinship ties and intricately overlapping claims to status and honor, quarrels were a constant fact of life, resulting in frequent bloodshed. Duels, vendettas, rebellions, and fratricidal war were an endemic feature of the Zhou order even at its most functional. In such a society, total peace was neither sought nor desired. Indeed, although the end results of violence were often mourned as regrettable, violence itself was celebrated as an inherent good.[15]

Given this intrinsic penchant for volatility, the Zhou domain cohered only because of the mechanisms that kept conflict within sustainable limits. Fear of the military retribution of the Zhou kings was one factor that conditionally inhibited violence. Another was the dual material and intangible gains that could be acquired through ceremonial interaction rather than brute force. The religious traditions of the Zhou made it possible for aristocratic adversaries to come together in shared rituals, where gifts might be exchanged, common ancestors worshipped, or oaths sworn. In this way, not only could aggrieved honor be restored but ties of kinship and allegiance could be formed or affirmed and symbolic prestige acquired, all of which were forfeited by the choice of arms. The sacral and ceremonial institutes of Zhou rule thus elevated the opportunity cost of violence high enough to prevent a wholesale breakdown of trust and good order.

This dynamic homeostasis began to disintegrate in the third and fourth centuries of Zhou rule. The Zhou's home base in the Wei River valley put them on the far western frontier of their own domain, causing constant tension between the opposing imperatives of defending against non-Chinese peoples to the west and projecting force eastward to keep peace among the vassal lords. In 771 B.C.E., this strain, combined with poor leadership, led to military catastrophe: the Zhou capital was overrun by an Inner Asian people known as the Xianyun. The Zhou kings were forced to flee eastward and take up residence on the Yellow River plain, in the midst of the territories of their vassals.[16]

At this eastern capital, the Zhou kings persisted at the sufferance of the surrounding lords, bereft of the economic and military assets with which they had once kept the king's peace. Order among the denizens of the Zhou domain now had to be maintained solely through the ritual institutions that could foster trust and sublimate violence. Overuse of these symbolic instruments led naturally to their debasement over time, as did the demographic pressure of an aristocracy that grew faster than the available fund of land and economic resources to support it. As the ceremonies and rites of the Zhou kings lost motive power, the warrior-aristocrats of the Zhou world turned ever more frequently to violence to settle conflicts.

This violence naturally escalated in intensity over time. There had been more than one hundred vassal lords scattered across the Zhou domain at the beginning of the dynasty; by the fifth century B.C.E., through conquest and annexation, more than two-thirds of those regional states had been swallowed up by neighboring rivals, and their number continued to fall. The polities that survived this destructive contest emerged vastly transformed. They controlled much more territory and had far greater resources than they had had previously, and because the stakes of warfare were now ultimately high, they sought new ways to maximize the military potential of their realms. At the beginning of the Zhou, warfare had been conducted by small armies of chariot-mounted aristocrats and had been constrained by myriad ceremonial protocols and taboos. By the fifth century B.C.E., states had begun to field large armies of conscript infantry, a trend that was accelerated by the invention of the crossbow. This new type of army was engaged in actions aimed less at honor or prestige and more at the acquisition of resources and the unrestrained destruction of the enemy's armed forces.[17]

It was in response to this shift in the nature and objectives of military action that the military writings of the Warring States period were produced. Although a new type of military had evolved in pursuit of new goals, the men who held power in the Zhou world continued to subscribe to the aristocratic mores of the Bronze Age. The persistent adherence to aristocratic values on the field of battle produced disastrous results. A new ethos was required to bring the role of the commander into alignment with the new operational parameters of the Warring States military. The authors of the military texts endeavored to fulfill this need.

Most fascinating about these military writings is that they arose in opposition to two powerfully entrenched interests that held sway over the small community of Warring States literati. On the one hand, the military writers were agitating against some of the most cherished values on which the self-image of the era's aristocratic rulers and elites was built. On the other hand, these authors were defying the emerging conventions of the literati community itself.

Thus when the first military writings appeared in the fourth century B.C.E., they emerged into a climate in which both political and cultural leaders were ill disposed to receive a message of military reform, though for different reasons. These social and cultural pressures conditioned the military texts that were produced in response to the crisis of the Warring States, a phenomenon that can be clearly seen in what is perhaps one of the earliest and certainly most outstanding examples of the genre: the *Sunzi bingfa*.[18]

It is widely acknowledged that the *Sunzi bingfa* could not have been written by its putative author, Sun Wu. Sun Wu was a commander famous for having led the armies of the southern state of Wu in successive victorious campaigns against the neighboring kingdoms of Chu and Yue in the sixth century B.C.E. The text of the *Sunzi* makes reference to technologies that did not exist during the historical Sun Wu's lifetime, such as the crossbow, and describes battlefield conditions, such as the deployment of conscript mass-infantry armies rather than teams of aristocratic chariots, that did not prevail until the Warring States period.[19] The *Sunzi* is thus the work of (a) Warring States author(s)[20] who assumed the identity of a figure that had lived at least two centuries before the composition of the text. Why?

The *Sunzi*'s highly polemical nature is often overlooked in critical commentary. Virtually all of the text's assertions were profoundly provocative in the society in which it first appeared. The opening of the *Sunzi* places it squarely in opposition to the traditional ethos of the aristocracy: "The military is the great affair of the state, the terrain of life and death, the Way of survival and extinction, it cannot but be investigated."[21] This is a reworking of an old adage that neatly encapsulated the aristocratic worldview: "The great affairs of the state are sacrifice and warfare."[22] Sacrifice underpinned the aristocracy's claims to social supremacy because it was conducted to their own ancestral spirits, reinforcing their assertion of exalted lineage. Warfare provided the opportunity to display courage and garner honor and itself served as a form of blood sacrifice in the service of the spirits. Military and spiritual matters were thus indissolubly linked from the perspective of the aristocracy: they viewed the battlefield as a sacred space within which what transpired was as much religious as it was tactical in nature.[23] The *Sunzi's* opening line rejects this perspective. All mention of sacrifice is eliminated, telegraphing the text's contention that martial matters must be viewed in purely material terms. Rather than "warfare," "the military" is held up as the great affair of the state, implying (as the text goes on to elaborate) that there are uses for military power beyond the "honorable" contest of arms. Moreover, the word that the *Sunzi* uses by reference to the "military," *bing*, does not evoke the aristocratic charioteer but the common foot soldier, who had become the backbone of the Warring States army.

The degree to which the *Sunzi* sets out to revolutionize the social conceptualization of military affairs can be perceived in the contrast between it and texts that express the conventional attitudes of the Bronze Age. For example, in the *Mencius* we see this celebration of martial valor very typical of the ethos of the Bronze Age aristocracy:

The way Bogong You cultivated his courage was by never showing submission on his face or letting anyone outstare him. For him, to yield the tiniest bit was as humiliating as to be cuffed in the market place. He would no more accept an insult from a prince with ten thousand chariots than from a common fellow coarsely clad. He would as soon run a sword through the prince as through the common fellow. He had no respect for persons, and always returned whatever harsh tones came his way.

Meng Shishe said this about the cultivation of his courage. "I look upon defeat as victory. One who advances only after sizing up the enemy, and joins battle only after weighing the chances of victory is simply showing cowardice in the face of superior numbers. Of course I cannot be certain of victory. All I can do is to be without fear."[24]

In contrast, the *Sunzi* makes this declaration, which was deeply offensive to the sensibilities of a warrior-aristocrat:

> If our officers have no extra wealth it is not because they hate possessions, if they have no further life span it is not because they hate longevity. On the day the orders are given those among the officers and men who are sitting will stain their coats with tears, those lying down will have tears cross their cheeks. Toss them into a place from which there is no escape and they will have the courage of a Zhuan Zhu or a Cao Gui.[25]

In an army made up of thousands of peasant conscripts who had no further to fall on the social scale, treating combat as a test of valor was not only logically absurd but also cataclysmically impractical. During the Bronze Age, when each combatant might lead an army of several hundred chariot-mounted aristocrats, a few warriors of conspicuous strength or bravery might make for a significant advantage. During the Warring States, however, when a typical army might be composed of tens of thousands of crossbowmen, the few individuals of exceptional courage served only to disrupt ranks that needed to stay closely arrayed for maximal tactical power. The new commander had to manipulate his forces on the assumption that they were, in aggregate, an army of cowards and count on them to behave that way from one tactical situation to the next.

The obsolescence of the ethos of heroic courage simultaneously entailed a complete reimagining of the conventions within which warfare transpired. In the aristocratic era, an absolute commitment to valor required adherence to an outmoded code of chivalry. The exploitation of tactical advantage was anathema to the aristocratic warrior, since it displayed cowardice and invited dishonor. A famous story exemplifies the pitfalls of this tradition:

> In winter, on the day *jisi*, the first day of the eleventh month, the Duke of Song did battle with the Chu troops by the Hong. When the

Song troops had already joined ranks, the Chu troops had not yet finished crossing. The Master of Horse said, "They are numerous and we are few; allow us to strike them before they have finished crossing." The duke said, "It is not permitted." When they had finished crossing but had not yet joined the ranks, he again reported it. The duke said, "It is not yet permitted." Striking them only after they had made formation, the Song army was routed. The duke was wounded in the thigh, and his gate officers were destroyed.[26]

In contrast, the *Sunzi* is unabashed in advocating the exploitation of any and every tactical or strategic advantage that can be acquired:

Emerge where he is not deployed, deploy where he does not expect. One who is not weary after moving one thousand *li* moves through empty territory. One whose attacks definitely succeed attacks where the enemy is not defending. One whose defense definitely succeeds defends what the enemy does not attack.[27]

Given the *Sunzi's* unequivocal embrace of tactical and strategic cunning, one might expect that its worldview would be correspondingly more "bloodthirsty" than that of the early aristocracy. The reality was more complicated, however. Although their idolization of courage bound the aristocracy to a chivalric code of combat, it also disposed them to view bloodshed as the necessary and spiritually fulfilling outcome of any armed encounter: the blood spilled on the battlefield served as proof of the combatants' common willingness to die and as a form of mass sacrifice to the ancestors and gods. From this perspective, warfare was not merely a ritual but *the* sacred template on which all other forms of ritual were in some sense based. This idea is expressed in an early text that describes the founding of the Zhou dynasty, the royal lineage that claimed rulership of the Sinic world during most of the Warring States:

King Wu had pursued and campaigned in the four directions. In all, there were 99 recalcitrant countries, 177,779 ears taken registered, and 310,230 captured men. . . . King Wu then sacrificed in the Zhou temple the ears taken of the many countries, declaring, "Reverently

I, the young son, slaughter six oxen and slaughter two sheep. The many states are now at an end." [He] reported in the Zhou temple, saying, "Of old I have heard that [my] glorious ancestors emulated the standards of the men of the Shang; with the dismembered body of [Shang king] Zhou, I report to heaven and to Ji [that is, Hou Ji]."[28]

Neither King Wu nor any Bronze Age aristocrat would have contemplated setting out on a major campaign without first reporting to and consulting the ancestral spirits in the clan temple. Nor could any campaign of conquest be deemed complete until, as in the case of King Wu, the victory was reported to the ancestors and the fruits of the battlefield offered up to them in a culminating round of sacrifices. War was, from beginning to end, a sacred devotional act, one to which bloodshed (as evidenced by the offering of the severed ears of the fallen) was indispensable.

From this early aristocratic perspective, the maxim for which the *Sunzi* is perhaps most famous, "To achieve one hundred victories in one hundred battles is not the supreme excellence, to reject battle and yet force the submission of the enemy's troops is the supreme excellence,"[29] is worse than nonsensical, it is offensive. To take up arms without shedding blood was sacrilege in the world of the Bronze Age aristocrat. The *Sunzi's* standard of excellence (like so much else in the text) plays havoc with the normative categories of the aristocratic ethos:

One who is victorious in battle and achieves no merit is ill augured; this is called wasted expense. Thus I say, "The enlightened ruler reflects upon it, the good commander studies it." If there is no profit, do not move, if there is no gain, do not employ [forces], if there is no danger, do not do battle. A ruler cannot mobilize the army from anger, a commander cannot join battle out of frustration. They move only in accord with profit and stop if no profit is to be had. Anger can revert to joy, frustration can revert to delight, but a destroyed state cannot be brought back into existence, the dead cannot be brought back to life.[30]

Where the aristocratic ethos located many of the benefits of warfare in a transcendent, spiritual dimension, the *Sunzi* insists that all assessments of military outcomes be made in purely material terms: "move only in accord with profit and stop if no profit is to be had." The character translated here as "profit," *li* 利, was unambiguous in its semantic implications. It represents a stalk of grain 禾 being cut by a knife 刀, and thus it could not be confused with any of the more intangible goods exalted in the spirit cult. Where King Wu could not imagine refusing his ancestors the ears of the fallen, the *Sunzi* would much rather have both the ears and the living soldiers attached to them pressed into the service of the commander and his sovereign. The distance between the former outlook and the latter is the gulf between different conceptual worlds. The *Sunzi* insists that *every* casualty of battle represents a loss for the victorious commander and his ruler: every friendly soldier killed was of course an asset lost, but every enemy soldier killed, every enemy provision destroyed, and every enemy fortification razed were also potential assets forfeited. This may seem self-evident to us reading the text today, but it represented a total intellectual revolution in the culture in which it was written.

This new scale of value for evaluating military outcomes established an indissoluble paradox at the heart of all military affairs, as is exemplified by the opening of chapter 2 of the *Sunzi*:

In the standards of employing the military, with one thousand fast chariots, one thousand armored chariots, one hundred thousand mailed infantry, carrying food for one thousand *li*, then the internal and external cash outlays, necessities for guest clients, supplies of glue and lacquer, provisions for chariots and infantry, will require a daily expenditure of one thousand [pieces of] gold. Only then can an army of one hundred thousand be mobilized. [Even] if it is used in battle and victorious, if [the campaign] is protracted then weapons will be blunted and morale diminished; if a walled city is assaulted then strength will be depleted. If the army is long engaged it will become impossible to meet the expenses of the state. . . . Thus one who makes protracted use of the military and profits the state has never been seen. If one does not completely understand the harm of using the military, one cannot completely understand the profit of using the military.[31]

The central irony of military affairs, from the new perspective of the *Sunzi*, is that the army consumed the very assets that it existed to defend and procure on behalf of the state. Moreover, the more actively and belligerently the army was employed, the faster it used up the very material profits on which the power of the state depended. Every potential use of the military thus had to be assessed with this paradox in mind. As soon as the army left the barracks, it began to consume one thousand pieces of gold per day; thus even in the case of a victorious campaign, if the ultimate gain to the state did not exceed the daily cost of keeping the army in the field, the outcome must be deemed worse than if the army had never been mobilized. Victory without fighting (through threats, trickery, or diplomacy) was the new optimum in this system of value, since it entailed none of the risks and inherent expense of old-fashioned combat.

The critical urgency of this imperative is underscored by the penultimate chapter of the *Sunzi*, "The Attack by Fire." Fire is a near-perfect Sunzian weapon, as the text declares in one of its more sardonically ironic turns of phrase: "One who assists the attack with fire is enlightened."[32] Fire's effectiveness cannot be undermined by the cowardice or ineptitude of one's own soldiers; it inflicts maximum destruction on the enemy while minimizing risks to one's own forces. By concluding its discussion of combat tactics with "The Attack by Fire," the *Sunzi* signals that this is the end toward which the inexorable logic of all warfare leads. Once the commitment to armed conflict has been made, in all likelihood it will force the choice between the extinction of one's own forces and the total, indiscriminate destruction of the enemy. For this reason, the resort to arms must be made only in the most exigent circumstances, as though it will inevitably entail great expense (one thousand pieces of gold per day from the moment the army sets foot out of the barracks); in the end, it may result only in the destruction of the assets that would have redeemed the cost of the campaign.

As it reconceptualizes the military and its ultimate purposes, the *Sunzi* also reinvents the role of the commander.[33] During the aristocratic era, the commander was chosen according to birth: leadership in the battle array was a position of hereditary privilege. During the Warring States, military command increasingly required an array of specialized skills and areas of knowledge, making it impossible to limit the choice of commander to a narrowly defined hereditary group. As the position of commander became one increasingly determined by merit, the need arose to rethink the principles guiding the ruler's assessment of the commander's performance. The aristocratic commander had not been called on to possess qualities radically different from that of any other noble warrior: he had to be brave and cut a good public figure. The *Sunzi*'s commander, by contrast, is enjoined to embrace a style and ethos directly opposed to that of the aristocratic warrior:

> [On] the day that an assault is undertaken, close the passes and break the tallies, do not admit [the enemy's] envoys. Stay strictly to the upper hall of the temple [厲于廊廟之上] in prosecuting the affair. When the enemy opens a breach, you must quickly enter it.... Thus be like a virgin girl at the outset. When the enemy opens a door, be like a darting rabbit in the end. The enemy will not be able to grasp you.[34]

Translators most often render the phrase 厲于廊廟之上 as "make *rigorous* [plans] in the upper temple hall."[35] But here the *Sunzi* is deploying gender markers to ironically underscore its assertions. The commander must at all cost avoid displays of martial bravado conventionally associated with the aristocratic warrior and instead remain *strictly* 厲 indoors and out of sight, as was the norm for unmarried women. This is the import of the injunction to "be like a virgin girl at the outset." A commander in the new military climate of mass-infantry warfare, asserts the *Sunzi*, adds value to the strategic enterprise only by accurately reading the enemy as one reads a text. All the while he must remain sensible, however, of the fact that every movement he himself makes is being observed by the enemy's spies and may yield critical information. Should this occur, then all the value the commander has added to the military endeavor is negated.

The structure of the text as a whole reinforces this general theme of the intellectual nature of command. The *Sunzi* begins with "Assessments" and ends with "The Employment of Spies," implicitly asserting that the task of command begins and ends with intellectual endeavors. The urgent role of the *Sunzi*'s commander resides in thought, not deeds. He is a gatherer and an analyzer of information rather than a bold hero or mighty combatant.

This dimension of the *Sunzi*'s message explains the choice of the text's author or authors to situate it in the "Masters' Literature" of the era. Over the Warring States, a large segment of the literati community came to be dominated by new but rapidly powerful cultural leaders: the Masters.[36] The first of these Masters was Confucius (551–479 B.C.E.), or "Master Kong." Confucius lived and taught in the militarily declining state of Lu; he was a low-level aristocrat (a *shi*, or "knight") who gathered young men around him as disciples.[37] Although there had been teachers before Confucius throughout the Zhou world, he elevated the position of teacher in his dealings with his disciples to a new level of moral and spiritual authority. His teachings were not confined to basic skills or even to the body of knowledge held in common by elite males. Confucius purported to instruct his students in the ultimate aims of learning, service, and even life itself, and to lead them in exploring the esoteric meanings that might be discovered in the cultural bequest of high antiquity. He presented his disciples with a total worldview and charged them, ultimately, with the salvation of Zhou civilization.

After Confucius's death, his disciples took on students of their own and became Masters in their own right, perpetuating the institution that Confucius had invented.[38] This model for the organization of intellectual life spread quickly throughout the Zhou world. As the field of active Masters proliferated, the range of opinions expressed by Masters on various subjects likewise became increasingly diverse; on the subject of military affairs, however, the teachings of the Masters were atypically consensual. Although there was some variation in their treatment of military matters, most Masters agreed that the military was a tainted subject that was beneath the dignity of genuine intellectual exploration.[39] Confucius was famously so offended at being asked a question about military affairs that he hastily departed the state of the ruler that had done so.[40] Master Mo (ca. 479–390 B.C.E.), who founded an entire tradition radically opposed to the teachings of Confucius, nevertheless shared Confucius's ambivalence toward military affairs. Among the basic tenets of his doctrine was a total ban on offensive warfare.[41] Song Xing (ca. 360–290 B.C.E.) and Yin Wen (ca. 350–285 B.C.E.), later Masters, took an even more radical stance than this, proposing that the military as an institution should be banned altogether.[42]

Some of this consensus can be attributed to the conditions of the time. Warfare was predictably viewed as the urgent pathology of the Warring States; thus those who arose to offer solutions for the problems of the era might naturally be inclined to look askance at military affairs. The near-total agreement of the Masters on this subject cannot be put down solely to intellectual concurrence, however. The social conditions that helped propel the spread of the Master–disciple organization itself also influenced the Masters' collective orientation toward military matters. As states became ever larger and more powerful, rulers (who over time eventually usurped the title of king, which had once belonged exclusively to the Zhou Son of Heaven) felt increasingly superior to and scornful of the stateless knights who accounted for the vast majority of literati. Under this and similar social pressures, the literati of the Warring States were naturally drawn toward the Master–disciple group, because it created a new universe of value within which knights could claim honor and dignity independent of their questionable aristocratic credentials.

This status insecurity on the part of the Masters and their disciples helps explain their broadly shared antipathy for military affairs. As discussed earlier, warfare had been one of the essential realms in which aristocrats had distinguished themselves and asserted their claims to social superiority during the early Zhou and ages prior. This cult of military valor persisted tenaciously, long outliving the historical conditions that had given it rational basis. Although the rulers of the enormous Warring States no longer personally engaged in combat on the field of battle, they continued to view themselves as warrior-aristocrats and to revere displays of martial prowess. For example, rulers lavished recognition and patronage on "wandering bravos" who traveled about and fought duels to win honor and fame for their expert swordsman-ship.[43] As long as such displays continued to be valued as marks of aris-tocratic distinction, the Masters and their disciples, who were engaged exclusively in civil pursuits, suffered by comparison. The Masters were thus spontaneously inclined, whatever their other disagreements, to embrace and exhort a worldview that asserted the superiority of *wen* over *wu*, the civil over the martial, as a way of defending their collec-tive claims to moral and intellectual leadership in the face of aristo-cratic social prejudices.[44]

Although from the very beginning the *Sunzi* identifies itself as the teachings of Master Sun, it just as immediately sets itself in opposition to the antimilitary conventions of the emerging Masters' Literature. As quoted earlier, the text begins by declaring that, far from being taboo or undignified, the military is "the great affair of the state," a subject that "cannot but be investigated." This radical contradiction of what had been the consensual Masters' position to that point helps explain the choice of Sun Wu as the putative author of the text. The com-poser of the *Sunzi* wanted to claim the same position of moral and intellectual authority established by other Masters but was cognizant of breaking ranks with other Masters' texts. He thus projected his own voice back in time, garnering legitimacy for his ideas by imbuing them with enhanced antiquity. Sun Wu was an older contemporary of Con-fucius's; thus by calling into existence "Master Sun," the *Sunzi bingfa* placed its concerns at the inception point of the Masters' corpus as a whole: as long as there had been Masters, there had been those will-ing to discuss military affairs. Moreover, Sun Wu's legend lent eerie prescience to the *Sunzi*'s opening assertion that the "Way of survival and extinction" resided in military affairs. As long as Sun Wu had com-manded its armies, his adoptive kingdom of Wu had thrived; but after his death, it was totally annihilated by the forces of Yue.[45]

Beyond merely broaching a subject that the emergent conventions of the Masters' discourse had construed as taboo, the *Sunzi* advanced theories that were profoundly troubling to a community largely com-mitted to the superiority of civil over military concerns. The basic teachings of the *Sunzi* did not entail merely a reconceptualization of the military, the commander, or the battlefield but also a larger reconceptualization of the state itself. The *Sunzi* placed the military at the foundation of the sovereign identity of the state. Historically (according to the *Sunzi*), the state had begun in tandem with the rise of military force, and in current times the state's existence was symbiotically tied to that of the military.[46] The military powers of the state were of such supreme importance that, while on campaign, the commander was not bound to follow the orders of even the ruler himself, becoming in effect a pro tempore king.[47]

Moreover, the *Sunzi*'s stress on the intelligence-gathering role of the commander broke down all distinction between the civil and military precincts of government. Spies might be recruited from any and all offices of the state, and since the commander had to take special care to "turn" spies who had been enlisted by the enemy,[48] his surveillance and manipulations necessarily extended to all government personnel even within his own kingdom, without regard to rank or function. Such formulations made it pragmatically impossible to ultimately distinguish between civil and military organs of the state, much less deem one superior to the other.

Given these dimensions of the *Sunzi*'s vision, its basic tenets were profoundly subversive of the doctrines propounded by the various Masters. Although the Masters vehemently disagreed with one another on many points of doctrine, they were united in the search for a transparently apprehensible standard of value that could serve as a basis for a new universal order. Confucius, for example, asserted that the world could be harmonized only by "rectifying names," rigorously identifying each phenomenon with the label that signified its role in the universally normative order (that is, only those who acted like proper rulers should be called rulers, only those who acted like proper sons should be called sons, and so on).[49] By contrast, in its opening chapter the *Sunzi* declares that "deception is the Way of the military."[50] The successful military commander never revealed the truth about himself, his plans, his forces, his ruler—indeed, about anything. He worked constantly to keep everyone about him in a state of confusion and misapprehension: total obfuscation rather than total transparency was his watchword. Although this principle ostensibly applied only within the realm of military affairs, because the *Sunzi* expanded the realm of military affairs to pervade all dimensions and functions of the state, the military's enjoinment to a program of perpetual deception precluded any and all hope of society's arriving at universally shared values.

Because the assertions of the *Sunzi bingfa* (and the other military texts that followed it) were so controversial in so many different precincts of Warring States society, they occasioned much resistance. This is especially evident in the Masters' texts of the period, which express overt hostility to this new perspective. The *Mencius* has its eponymous protagonist (Master Meng, or Mencius [ca. 390–305 B.C.E.]), declare,

> While he was steward to the Ji family, Ran Qiu doubled the yield of taxation without being able to improve their virtue. Confucius said, "Qiu is not my disciple. You, little ones, may attack him to the beating of drums." From this it can be seen that Confucius rejected those who enriched rulers not given to the practice of benevolent government. How much more would he reject those who do their best to wage war on their behalf. In wars to gain land, the dead fill the plains; in wars to gain cities, the dead fill the cities. This is known as showing the land the way to devour human flesh. Death is too light a punishment for such men. Hence those skilled in war should suffer the most severe punishments.[51]

This passage is somewhat abstract and could arguably be aimed at commanders and officials more generally rather than the proponents of specific texts. The allusion to Confucius's displeasure with his own disciple strongly suggests the context of an intellectual dispute, however. In the same way that Confucius was willing to break violently with Ran Qiu for his breach of principle, the authors of the *Mencius* signal their absolute antipathy toward those intellectuals, like the authors of the military texts, who were willing to treat war as a purely tactical or strategic problem, absent any regard for its moral context.

Although the *Mencius* only obliquely evinces any awareness of the emergent military literature, other Masters' texts soon demonstrated a clear familiarity with the genre. The *Xunzi*, which bears the name of Confucius's second great latter-day disciple, Xun Qing (ca. 310–

220 B.C.E.), contains an entire chapter entitled "Debating the Military." The chapter purports to record an oral argument between the Lord of Linwu and Xunzi himself, held in the presence of King Xiaocheng of Zhao (r. 265–244 B.C.E.). During the debate, the Lord of Linwu espouses ideas that echo the perspective of new military texts such as the *Sunzi bingfa*:

> What the military values is force [*shi*] and profit [*li*], what it enacts is alterations and deception. The one who is skilled at using the military sows confusion and moves in darkness; none knows from whence he will emerge. Sun [Wu] and Wu [Qi] used [these means], and had no match in the world; what need is there to rely on the people?
>
> Master Xun Qing said, "Not so. What I take as the Way is the military [methods] of the humane person, the ambition of a [True] King. What you value—expediency and plotting, force and profit, attack and seizure, alteration and deception—are the affairs of the Lords of the Land."[52]

By the middle of the third century B.C.E., the *Sunzi bingfa* and other military texts had become broadly influential, so much so that even a hostile text such as the *Xunzi* was compelled to engage them. Although the *Xunzi* depicts its eponymous protagonist as the clear winner in the subsequent debate excerpted here, such a narrative did not reflect the actual trajectory of society at large. The military texts grew steadily more pervasive, so that by the time the Warring States were united under the Qin empire in 221 B.C.E., their authors, students, and proponents had completely remade the military culture of early China. Indeed, much of the conceptualization of the militarized imperial state that emerged from the Qin conquest might be attributed in part to the military texts.

By the time the *Huainanzi* was presented in 139 B.C.E., the military texts had gone from being incendiary and subversive literature to one among many genres of writing on affairs that were of concern to the state. The materialist, instrumentalist perspective of the *Sunzi bingfa* became all but hegemonic in military affairs; its notions of the ideal commander and the secular dynamics that ruled the battlefield were accepted as common wisdom. At the same time, the raw fact of unification had dramatically altered the military disposition of the Chinese social environment. The *Sunzi bingfa* had been written in a multipolar world and theorized about military affairs on that basis. In the absence of competing claims to sovereign legitimacy, some of the *Sunzi*'s abstract principles no longer mapped out well onto the conceptual universe of the imperial era.

All these developments are reflected in the *Huainanzi*'s treatment of military affairs, as can be seen by comparing "Bing lüe" with the brief excerpt from the *Xunzi* just quoted. "Bing lüe" shares none of the *Xunzi*'s aversion to the idea of *shi*, or "force," a basic conceptual tool developed by the *Sunzi bingfa* and other early military texts:

> Now let two people cross blades. If their skill or clumsiness is no different, the braver warrior will certainly win. Why is this? It is because of the sincerity of his actions. If you use a great ax on logs and firewood, you need not wait for a beneficial time or a good day to chop it. If you put the ax on top of the logs and firewood without the aid of human effort, though you accord with the "far-flight" asterism and have hold of recision and accretion, you will not chop it because there is no force.
>
> Thus,
>> when water is agitated, it dries up;
>> when an arrow is agitated, it flies far.
>
> The end of an arrow made of Qiwei bamboo and capped with silver and tin could not on its own pierce even a vest of thin silk or a shield of rotten leaves. If you lend it the strength of sinew and bone, the force of bow or crossbow, then it will pierce rhino[-hide] armor and pass through a leather shield!
>
> The speed of the wind can reach the point of blowing away roofs or breaking trees, [but] if an empty carriage reaches a great thoroughfare from atop a high hill, a person has pushed it. For this reason the force of one who is skilled at using arms is
>> like releasing amassed water from a thousand-*ren*[-high] dike,
>> like rolling round stones into a ten-thousand-*zhang*[-deep] gorge. (15.18)

This is among the most detailed and illustrative discussions of the concept of *shi* in early literature. The word itself has no precise equivalent in English. *Shi* is a measure of the combat effectiveness of a soldier, unit, formation, or position. As the preceding examples make clear, the versatility of *shi* for thinking through tactical situations derived from its integration of multiple variables into a single gauge. For example, in the case of the two swordsmen, the *shi* of each combatant encompasses all the intrinsic qualities that affect his performance. If the level of skill of both opponents is the same, greater courage will give the braver swordsman more *shi* and predictably lead to his victory.

Such intrinsic factors are not the only determinants of *shi*, however. Extrinsic contingencies can amplify or diminish the *shi* of a combatant or a weapon. Arrows and axes may be inherently capable of penetrating leather and wood, but they depend on the application of human agency to realize that potential. Water poses little threat when collected in a still pond, but amassed and released from a great height it becomes powerfully destructive. I thus translate *shi* as "force," because it is calculated along these intersecting intrinsic and extrinsic axes of power in the same way that, in physics, force subsumes the paired factors of mass and velocity.

The utility of force for military assessment and planning should be obvious. It facilitates the amalgamation of all contingencies that affect the disposition of opposing units into a single measurement. For example, a group of twenty archers will, all things being equal, have more force than a group of ten archers. This disparity could be leveled, however, if the smaller group was highly trained and the larger group was raw recruits. The force advantage could be tilted even more toward the smaller unit if it was placed on a hill while its opponents occupied a defile. Force was posited by the *Sunzi* and other early military texts as the paramount factor controlling the dynamics of the battlefield, totally displacing the will of the spirits and the relative moral qualities of the combatants. It afforded the commander a tool with which to model a conflict in logical and quantifiable terms: calculate which side of the contest possessed more force (taking into account all variables), and the outcome was transparently predictable.

The concept proved so versatile that it quickly migrated into other realms of language and inquiry. Statecraft theorists such as Shen Dao wrote of the *shi* possessed by individual members of a hierarchical political structure, stressing the destabilizing consequences if the actual *shi* of an official surpassed that of his nominal superiors (in such contexts, *shi* translates less awkwardly into English as "political advantage" rather than "force," though the principle underpinning both meanings is the same).[53] Beyond these technical usages, because *shi*, like force, always has both magnitude and direction, it was appropriated to describe the inherent propensity or trajectory of things or situations. For example, it is the *shi* of a ball to roll; it is the *shi* of a poorly led state to grow more chaotic.[54]

The broadening currency of the concept of force demonstrates the degree to which the military texts of the Warring States helped revolutionize thinking about not only military affairs but also politics, social dynamics, and the world more generally. As the *Xunzi* demonstrates, this revolution did not transpire without resistance, at least initially. The idea of force distressed the authors of the *Xunzi* and other like-minded intellectuals because it operated in completely amoral terms, creating a scale of assessment independent of and potentially in competition with the ethical norms promulgated by Masters' texts like the *Analects* (*Lun yu*), *Mencius*, *Xunzi*, and *Mozi*.

The success of armies guided by the new thinking of the military texts eventually forced a paradigm shift in the cultural realm, however. Although the quoted passage from the *Huainanzi* stresses the human dimension of the generation of force, it deploys the concept as it was constructed by texts such as the *Sunzi*. Elsewhere, "Bing lüe" describes three types of force that prevail on the battlefield: the force of *qi*, the force of terrain, and the force of circumstance. The first is the internal energy possessed by troops as a result of their level of morale, while the latter two are extrinsic contingencies that can enhance or impede combat effectiveness. To these forms of force the *Huainanzi* adds a second calculation, *quan*. The word *quan* originally denoted the weight used in conjunction with a steelyard or set of balanced scales. "Bing lüe" uses it to signify the prior preparations that influence a combatant before battle is engaged that can potentially "tip the scales" on the field. For this reason, I translate *quan* as "heft." The *Huainanzi* identifies two forms of heft: the knowledge of the commander and the training of his soldiers. Once all forms of force and heft have been accounted for, the outcome of a battle can be known in advance:

> If arms are not sure to be victorious, one does not rashly cross blades;
> if the assault is not sure to take [its object], one does not rashly launch [it].
> Only after victory is certain does one give battle;
> only after the scales have been weighed does one move. (15.13)[55]

Here the echo of early military texts like the *Sunzi* can clearly be heard. The *Huainanzi* (unlike the *Xunzi*) completely assents to the *Sunzi's* new model of the ideal commander and the battlefield over which he presides. The battlefield is not a ritual arena or spiritual realm but a secular space within which measurable dynamics can be examined, quantified, and manipulated. Correspondingly, the commander is not a martial hero or noble champion but a skilled expert whose merit is earned through knowledge and planning. These shifts in perspective do not represent the ideological preferences of the *Huainanzi's* authors so much as structural changes in the military culture of the Chinese world that had been transpiring since even before the *Xunzi* was written. By the time the *Huainanzi* was presented to Emperor Wu, the command concept of texts like the *Sunzi bingfa* was increasingly becoming the norm by which military personnel were recruited and assessed.[56]

In similar ways, certain departures of "Bing lüe" from the perspective of the Warring States military texts were induced by the changing geostrategic circumstances of the imperial era. The Han ruled over a united polity that had been divided into seven competing independent kingdoms at the time that the *Sunzi bingfa* had been written. In these new circumstances, the *Sunzi's* stress on profit as a central principle motivating the military and its use by the state became philosophically problematic. When the chief mission of the military had been the survival of the state in conflict with matched opponents, the husbanding and acquisition of resources was a natural corollary of the military's objective. But in a new era in which the imperial state stood alone and unchallenged within the Chinese domain, orienting the military toward profit appeared more as rapine than good strategic sense.

This switch in perspective is made starkly manifest in the very opening line of "Bing lüe": "In antiquity, those who used the military did not value expanding territory or covet the possession of gold and jade" (15.1). Throughout the text, there is no reference to the central paradox of military affairs established by the *Sunzi*: the fact that in using the military, the state expends the very resources that the military exists to defend and accumulate. Indeed, "Bing lüe" reconceptualizes the military and its raison d'être in ways that negate the *Sunzi's* paradox altogether.

"Bing lüe," in keeping with the general tenor of military culture in the Han, imagines the military on a strictly "nonprofit" basis. Since the Han recognized no legitimate sovereign authority completely independent from the imperial throne, the military existed only to curb and punish those who did not comply with the imperial mandate. Even functions that we in the twenty-first century might identify as aspects of foreign policy fell within this punitive brief. Although non-Chinese peoples such as the Xiongnu tribesman of the northern steppe were pragmatically independent of Han authority, Han political ideology deemed them theoretical subjects of the Han emperor; thus even defensive campaigns to repel Xiongnu raids and invasions were, in principle, punishments for acts of rebellion. The *Sunzi's* stress on profit had made sense only when the military was conceived of as a genuine foreign policy arm of the state. In the imperial era, the military necessarily became, in theory at least, wholly subsumed within the judicial organs of the government, and thus profit was no longer an adaptive principle around which to structure its function.[57]

Other historical developments likewise inflect the treatment in "Bing lüe" of military affairs. In the process of becoming "mainstream," the corpus of military writings had grown exponentially and became very diverse in content, style, and subject matter. Military culture evolved in directions paralleling the movement of culture more generally. One outstanding development was the accelerated popularity of "yin-yang Five Phases" cosmological thought, a mode of discourse that made its mark on all intellectual activity in the early imperial period. A large literature on the military applications of correlative cosmological theory developed, and military men were expected to have some familiarity with its principles and practices.[58]

To our twenty-first-century sensibilities, this might seem like a corrupting admixture of "mysticism" to the highly rational and skeptical discourse established by the *Sunzi* and other early texts. Such a judgment is a distortion, however. Although it always had its skeptics, correlative cosmology was conceived as operating in purely secular and material terms. Correlative processes were driven by the phenomenon of *ganying*, or "resonance." Because all things in the universe were made of *qi*, stimulating any one thing in the cosmos would create a simultaneous response in other objects (or people) composed of corresponding types of *qi*. A person who understood the patterns according to which these constantly operative resonant influences were exchanged could foretell the future or extrapolate conditions transpiring far away.[59] This mode of inquiry and prognostication was generally perceived by early Chinese thinkers themselves as more rational and empirical than the attribution of causes and effects to the workings of ancestors or spirits. Although cosmological texts did, in some sense, depart from the perspective of the *Sunzi*, they affirmed its stress on the intellectual faculties of the commander. Correlative cosmology created a new universe of technical knowledge, the mastery of which could further distinguish the commander as a learned expert.

The authors and compilers of the *Huainanzi* were, like most intellectuals of their era, fascinated with correlative cosmology and its various applications. They included an entire chapter in the first section of the book, "Surveying Obscurities" (chapter 6), which describes the basic mechanism of correlative cosmology and argues for its importance in the curriculum of the sage-ruler. Cosmological themes and ideas are woven throughout the other sections of the text, and "Bing lüe" is no exception. At several points, the chapter declares that cosmological lore must be within the scope of the successful commander's learning; for example, "When one is clear as to freak occurrences and anomalies, yin and yang, recision and accretion, the Five Phases, the observance of *qi*, astrology, and spirit supplication, this is to be skillful at the Way of Heaven" (15.24).

At other points, "Bing lüe" assigns cosmic resonance a central and determinative role in the conduct of military affairs (discussed further in the following). "Bing lüe" does not, however, delve into the specific content of applied cosmological lore in any depth; there is no discussion of how one "observes *qi*" or forecasts events on the basis of the stars. This is in part due to the pedagogical perspective of the text as a whole; it is not designed for a field commander but for a young emperor who will have to oversee military affairs. It thus does not enumerate technical details but gives the general terms and concepts that would be useful to following the discussion of military matters at court.

This is not the only reason, however, for the superficial treatment in "Bing lüe" of applied cosmology. As the conclusion of section 15.24 states of cosmology and other forms of technical knowledge, though "one cannot lack even one of these . . . they are not what is most valuable to the military." This assertion expresses a basic ideological perspective of the *Huainanzi* as a whole and underscores an important aspect of the *Huainanzi*'s treatment of military affairs. Although the bones and sinews of "Bing lüe" are drawn from the military textual tradition of the Warring States, it distinguishes itself from those earlier writings in ways that are not always explicable as the product of changing times. "Bing lüe" is not merely a Warring States military tract transposed to the imperial age; it projects a distinctive and original vision of military affairs that reflects its authors' and patron's particular political interests and ideological preferences. To understand these unique dimensions of the text, we must explore the other contexts that influenced its production and reception.

Root and Branches 本末: "Bing lüe" in the *Huainanzi*

"Bing lüe" is the fifteenth chapter of the *Huainanzi*, a fact that provides essential clues to the text's overall treatment of its subject matter.

The central problem confronting the authors of the *Huainanzi* was the challenge of coherence. The intellectual culture of the multipolar Warring States world was vibrantly diverse; it produced a wide array of mutually conflicting traditions of thought, practice, and inquiry. The Qin, the first imperial dynasty to unify the former Zhou domain, attempted to radically simplify the ideological basis of imperial rule. The private study of all but a narrow range of texts was banned. Privately held copies of proscribed texts had to be surrendered to the state for incineration, and scholars caught in possession of banned manuscripts were buried alive in retribution.[60] Needless to say, these policies caused widespread resentment and were further discredited by the cataclysmic implosion of the dynasty itself in the immediate aftermath of the First Emperor's death.

Upon inheriting the imperial state structure created by the Qin, the rulers of the Han dynasty were at pains to avoid committing Qin's mistakes and sharing in its dismal reputation. The Han founder, Liu Bang, and his successors were ecumenically tolerant of all the various (and often mutually contradictory) traditions of thought passed down from the Warring States. Indeed, in its early decades, the court culture of the Han had an improvisational character as Han rulers and officials freely adopted doctrines and practices on an ad hoc basis, according to the perceived needs of the moment.[61]

As Han institutions matured, however, a growing need was perceived for a more consistent and coherent set of doctrines and practices to guide the ongoing operation of the Han court. The free-form political culture of the early Han created a climate of uncertainty surrounding policy decisions and personnel matters, leading to factional infighting and hindering the efficient functioning of the state. Even as the need for coherence grew more urgent, however, the negative example of the Qin still favored a more open and inclusive approach to the construction of imperial doctrine. There was broad sympathy for retaining as much of the bequest of classical antiquity as possible. This was not a purely academic matter, moreover. Literati were employed by the Han court on the merits of the textual traditions in which they claimed particular expertise. If a text was excluded from the imperial curriculum, its students and adherents were thus effectively excluded from state service. A call for intellectual inclusiveness was therefore simultaneously a call to broaden the opportunities for service in the imperial state and to reconcile the ideological factions that had been locked in competition over control of imperial policy.[62]

This imperative for inclusiveness, however, posed the vexing problem of how to harmonize the diverse and mutually discordant teachings of the Warring States. Other attempts had been made to syncretize the contending traditions of the Masters. The most important of these in terms of its influence on the *Huainanzi* was the *Lüshi chunqiu*, a text composed and compiled by scholars working under the patronage of Lü Buwei, a prime minister of the state of Qin shortly prior to unification.[63] A Qin calendrical date inscribed at the end of the first section of the text indicates that it was at least partially completed in 239 B.C.E., eighteen years before Qin conquered the other Warring States and founded the unified empire.[64]

Lü Buwei's text showed a very different face to the Chinese world than would eventually prevail at the court of the First Emperor. Where the First Emperor imposed a reductively statist ideology on his united empire, Lü Buwei patronized scholars adhering to a wide array of traditions and produced a text that preserved the distinctive voice and perspective of each. Although the work thus necessarily contained much mutually contradictory advice, Lü and his clients hit on an organizational principle that lent the text overall coherence.

As is indicated in the postface to "The Twelve Records," the first of three sections into which the *Lüshi chunqiu* was divided, the structure of the text replicated the basic and irreducible categories composing the structure of the entire universe. The text's three main divisions embodied the threefold division of the cosmos between Heaven, Earth, and Humankind. Each of these divisions was further subdivided into sections embodying aspects and forces inherent in the cosmic realm to which it corresponded. For example, "The Twelve Records," the section corresponding to Heaven, was divided into twelve books for the twelve months of the calendar year, each of which was divided into five chapters corresponding to the five phases of *qi*. These chapters then placed the teachings of various Masters within the seasonal position most thematically appropriate: teachings on vitality and longevity reminiscent of Master Yang Zhu in the spring, teachings on education and maturity reminiscent of Confucius in the summer, and so on. In this way, the seeming inconsistencies of the Masters' teachings could be reconciled as expressions of underlying cosmic realities. All the Masters had discovered only a portion of the unitary cosmic truth, but the *Lüshi chunqiu* had reconstituted that perfect Way by slotting each Master's teachings into the cosmic context to which it was appropriate. The text thus presented a powerful argument that the Masters' doctrines and practices could be made to work together just as such mutually conflicting cosmic processes as heat and cold, summer and winter, life and death work together.

This was an innovative use of the overall structure of a text, the first of its kind in the world of early Chinese letters. Although Lü Buwei was disgraced, exiled, and driven to suicide shortly after the completion of his great text, it was preserved and was widely influential in the early empire.[65] Qin ultimately repudiated Lü's vision, but the *Lüshi chunqiu* did accomplish its rhetorical aim: to demonstrate that political unification could be facilitated by intellectual unification; that all the traditions of thought and inquiry developed in the Warring States could be harnessed to the use of a new imperial state.

Although the *Lüshi chunqiu* presented a vision of unity, it was somewhat provisional and tenuous. Demonstrating that the complexity of the cosmos could be paralleled by a multifaceted political doctrine left many questions unanswered. The ideas and techniques of the Masters were each shown to have a place in the *Lüshi chunqiu*'s grand synthesis, but the text's scheme did not indicate which were more and which were less essential, or provide ready criteria by which the correct technique or doctrine could be chosen and applied on a case-by-case basis.

In convening his guest scholars and setting them to the composition of the *Huainanzi*, Liu An was clearly acting in emulation of Lü Buwei. Liu and his clients aimed for a higher degree of coherence in their grand summa, however. In the last chapter of the text, "An Overview of the Essentials," they declared that they had achieved a final and perfect reconciliation of the traditions of the classical age, one that could serve as a timeless doctrine for the Han dynasty and its imperial mission.[66] In making this claim, the *Huainanzi* used a similar mechanism to that employed by the *Lüshi chunqiu*: it posited a basic structural correspondence between the operations of the cosmos and the institutions of human culture and society. The principles on which the *Huainanzi* made this argument, however, were unique. The *Huainanzi* asserted that the evolution, structure, and ongoing operation of the entire cosmos were determined by a dynamic principle it labeled "root and branches." Every fundamental realm of existence — matter, energy, the mind, the body, human history, society, culture, politics — embodied this root–branches principle.[67]

At basis, the root–branches concept was inspired by chapter 42 of the *Laozi*, which states that "the One gave birth to the Two, the Two gave birth to the Three, the Three gave birth to the myriad things." In other words, the universe began as a Grand Unity; at the origin, all that existed was a vast field of undifferentiated primal *qi*. The first step in cosmogenesis was the differentiation of that primal *qi* into the two polarities of yin and yang. Yin and yang then interacted to create the Five Phases, and these interacted to create the diverse and complex world in which we live.

As the posterior forms of *qi* and matter emerged, however, they did not separate from the Grand Unity. Although the universe appears diverse, its component "parts" are only distinguishable by contrast with one another. Moreover, all things in the universe are constantly engaged in a cycle of dynamic transformation and periodically break down and return to the state of primordial *qi*. Thus although an object may appear distinct right now, one is viewing only a temporary interval between returns to the undifferentiated primordial state. All things are thus ultimately a part of the Grand Unity from which they emerge and to which they inevitably return.

The Grand Unity from which all things emerged is virtually synonymous with what the *Laozi* and other texts call the Dao, or the Way.[68] The Way is the origin, totality, and driving dynamism of the cosmos, encompassing everything that is, was, or might be. Nothing can persist outside it; thus it cannot be apprehended in language, which requires the possibility of contrast. All contingent phenomena emanate from the Way and are impelled by it in their functioning and transformation.[69]

The key to power in this universe is to understand the root–branches pattern by which it came into being. The Way is the root; all contingent phenomena are branches. The closer in origin a phenomenon is to the cosmic root and the less differentiated it is from the pristine Grand Unity, the more replete it is with latent potential and dynamic potency. For example, in order to control affairs in the world, harnessing the power of Heaven and Earth is excellent, because they were among the first phenomena to emerge from the Grand Unity and are thus extraordinarily powerful. Even better, however, is to harness the power of the Way, as it preceded Heaven and Earth and is limitlessly potent.

This root–branches pattern is not confined to cosmogony, moreover, but is replicated at every level of existence. Because all things emerge from the Way, all things embody the same root–branches trajectory in their evolution and function. The human being begins as a protean embryo, and from that featureless root grows organs and limbs.[70] Human consciousness begins in empty stillness and develops the "branches" of thought, perception, and feeling only when stimulated by external things.[71] At the macro level, human society began as an ultimately simplistic collectivity and developed technology, social structures, cultural forms, and political institutions only as it grew more diverse and complex over time.[72] It is these structural homologies that the *Huainanzi* draws between cosmic, natural, and human history that inform the text's grand synthesis of the classical cultural tradition. All the doctrines and practices promulgated by the Masters were laid out by the text along a developmental continuum, prioritized according to the order in which they emerged during the long sweep of cosmic time.

At the very beginning of human history, it had been possible to rule humanity using only the Way and its Potency. The Way is thus the root of not only all cosmic but also all political order and must be relied on as the single, indispensable foundation of any successful system of government. As society evolved, however, it became necessary for ancient sage-rulers to supplement the Way and its Potency with values like Humaneness and Rightness. These values thus likewise became indispensable to successful rule in their own and subsequent eras but remained less fundamental and essential than the Way and its Potency in ultimate terms. As both the cosmos and society continued to grow more complex, new implements of order became necessary. When the Way, its Potency, Humaneness, and Rightness were no longer sufficient to the task of good order, sages created ritual and music to supplement them. When ritual and music likewise proved wanting as mechanisms of rule, sages created standards, measurements, laws, and punishments.

The key to good order in any given era is thus to understand the correct root–branches relationship between the various mechanisms of control at the ruler's disposal. As time passed, the task of government became inexorably more complex, precluding the possibility of "turning the clock back" and resorting only to the implements of a former, simpler age.[73] At the same time, placing one's faith in latter-day devices and techniques while ignoring or discarding the more fundamental resources of high antiquity was a recipe for disaster.

This root–branches conceptual scheme explained (from the text's own perspective) not only why the *Huainanzi* was able to reconcile the teachings of the classical Masters but also why it had surpassed and could displace all earlier teachers. The Confucians, for example, were shown to be hopelessly misguided, since they foolishly privileged an arbitrarily narrow band of the full root–branches spectrum necessary to good order. They placed ultimate value in Humaneness and Rightness, which was to rely on a branch phenomenon and abandon the deeper root of the Way and its Potency. At the same time, they valued rites and music to the exclusion of laws and punishments, which was to cling hopelessly to the implements of an earlier time and neglect the necessary technologies of latter days. By contrast, the Qin rulers, who had embraced laws and punishments but scorned Humaneness and Rightness, were less conservative but no less foolish, since their total reliance on tertiary branch phenomena had been destined for self-subversion and collapse.

This root–branches vision not only informed the doctrinal perspective of the *Huainanzi* but determined its overall structure as well. The first chapter of the text is "Originating in the Way," and thus it begins at the very root of the universe and all the phenomena it contains. It then proceeds, chapter by chapter, through progressively less fundamental realms in the order in which they emerged from Grand Unity: Potency (chapter 2, "Activating the Genuine"), Heaven (chapter 3, "Celestial Patterns"), Earth (chapter 4, "Terrestrial Forms"), time (chapter 5, "Seasonal Rules"), resonance (chapter 6, "Surveying Obscurities"), the human mind and body (chapter 7, "Quintessential Spirit"), and so forth. The farther one reads past chapter 1, the more distant one becomes from the root and the more deeply one enters into the branches of its contents.

It is thus highly significant that "Bing lüe," the text's chapter on military affairs, appears in the position of fifteen, for it marks military matters as a clearly branch concern in both synchronic and diachronic ways. All the elements of rule that appear in earlier chapters, such as ritual (chapter 11, "Integrating Customs"), came into existence earlier in human history. Many early rulers had been able to govern in the total absence of coercive force; thus arms are a late, devolutionary development in the unfolding of history and must be ranked below earlier, more pristine expressions of human beings' cosmic potential. In latter days, although arms have become an indispensable implement of rule, their use and function must remain peripheral to the task of governance if good order is to be maintained. The normative quality and long-term sustainability of a government can be measured in the extent to which its exercise of power is carried out through nonmilitary means. In a potentially successful realm, noncoercive means of control such as ritual, music, and the mysterious resonant influence of the ruler's Potency are far more central to the function of government than the application of military force.

Given this larger context of the military's place within the root–branches continuum established by the *Huainanzi* as a whole, Edmund Ryden's characterization of "Bing lüe" as expressing "a philosophy of peace, not pacifism" is accurate.[74] The text establishes a basic feedback principle: war is rightly waged only in the ultimate pursuit of peace. At the same time, however (as Ryden notes), the text acknowledges that in a world grown more complex a certain minimum threshold of conflict is unavoidable. Peace will not be maintainable in the absence of arms; in latter days, even a perfect ruler will need to use the sword. Total disarmament is thus not possible, and the occasional recourse to arms does not necessarily entail a shortfall from the sage ideal.

The principle that Ryden so elegantly distills does not tell the whole story, however. To stop at interpreting "Bing lüe" as expressing the value of peace in the abstract misses much that is of interest in the text. The overall doctrine of the *Huainanzi* undeniably informed the perspective of "Bing lüe," and there is little reason to doubt that Liu An and his guest scholars were sincerely men of peace. At the same time, however, the unique treatment of military affairs laid out in chapter 15 of the *Huainanzi* coincides with the political and personal interests of Liu An in ways too obvious to ignore. Although "Bing lüe" is a branch chapter, the subject of military affairs touched on vital and hotly contested issues that influenced the position of the text's patron within the imperial structure of the Han dynasty. The chapter thus provided Liu An with an urgent venue for arguments and assertions on which the future of his court as a political enterprise might hinge.

One cannot fully understand "Bing lüe" without understanding the ways in which its discussion of military affairs worked to the particular advantage of Liu An and his court. This dimension of the text is of extreme interest, moreover, because it cannot be dismissed as a merely cynical and disingenuous manipulation of the issues to self-serving ends. Liu An's position within the Han structure as a whole gave him a unique and legitimate perspective, and even as the ideas forwarded in "Bing lüe" served Liu An's interests, they also posed pragmatic solutions to genuine problems confronting the imperial state. With these factors in mind, I now turn to a reading of "Bing lüe" within the geopolitical context of the court of Huainan.

Sustain the Perishing, Revive the Extinct 存亡繼絕: "Bing lüe" and the Court of Huainan

Edmund Ryden notes that in its opening lines, "Bing lüe" describes the normatively correct military of antiquity as bound to "pacify the chaos of the world, and eliminate the harm to the myriad people." But in identifying this "philosophy of peace," Ryden elides an even more prominent and recognizable declaration that precedes this general call to pacification, one that would have been familiar to every educated reader during Han times:

> In antiquity, those who used the military did not value expanding territory or covet the possession of gold and jade. They sought to *sustain those who [were] perishing, revive those [lineages] that had been cut off*, pacify the chaos of the world, and eliminate harm to the myriad people. (15.1)

The phrases in italics were an oft-quoted maxim found throughout the Masters' texts and exegetical literature of the Warring States and early Han.[75] In classical Chinese, this formula is rhythmically succinct, only four characters long: *cun wang ji jue* 存亡繼絕. The grammar is quite idiosyncratic. *Wang* and *jue*, used here as nouns, usually appear as verbs: "to perish," "to be cut off." *Cun* and *ji* are most often intransitive verbs, "to survive" and "to continue"; thus it is rare to see them take a direct object in this way. Moreover, when *cun* and *wang* are paired, it is almost invariably as opposed antonyms, as in the famous phrase at the opening of the *Sunzi bingfa*: "the Way of survival and extinction." To see *wang* nominalized as the object of *cun* is unique. All this is to say that this maxim had a very particular and commonly recognized meaning, one for which it was very deliberately chosen and placed at this prominent point in the text.

The meanings and implications of this dictum were complex, rooted in debates that had been ongoing for centuries before the composition of the *Huainanzi*. In the earliest Warring States Masters' writings in which it appeared, "sustain the perishing, revive the extinct" specifically described the virtuous policy of the *ba*, or "hegemons," especially the first lord to wield that title, Duke Huan of Qi, and his chief minister, Guan Zhong.[76] The *Guanzi* (*Master Guan*) describes how Duke Huan, on Guan's advice, made "sustaining the perishing, reviving the extinct" the guiding principle for his conduct as hegemon.[77] The "perishing" and "extinct" were not abstractions in this sense but specifically signified vassal houses that, though holding hereditary charters from the Zhou kings, either were in danger of being destroyed or had already been cut off in their line of succession. Duke Huan reportedly made it his mission to rescue such houses if they had not already been made extinct, or to find means of reviving the sacrificial cult of houses whose ancestral temples had already been destroyed.[78]

This was key, according to the *Guanzi*, to the legitimacy of the hegemon's (and, by extension, any sovereign's) use of coercive power. Violence against a particular vassal lord was justifiable only if the ultimate continuation of each vassal house's line of succession was held sacrosanct. No matter how extreme the destructiveness of a campaign, an assailant could not be accused of pursuing self-enrichment if he was committed to reconstituting the ancestral cult of his opponent in the wake of his opponent's demise. As the Warring States progressed, this principle of "sustaining the perishing, reviving the extinct" was accepted by many texts as the litmus test for the legitimate use of coercive force. Although by the Warring States the title of hegemon no longer held currency, by celebrating earlier hegemons' dedication to "sustaining the perishing and reviving the extinct," Warring States authors declared that there were clear moral and spiritual constraints to the naked exercise of coercive power.

By the early Han, this message had been further amplified by the concept's association with Confucius in the exegetical tradition to the *Spring and Autumn Annals*. The *Annals* was a year-by-year chronicle of the state of Lu, Confucius's home state, from 722 to 481 B.C.E. Confucians deemed it the personal work of Confucius himself and posited that Confucius had woven subtle language into its terse entries and pronouncements from which one could deduce his normative judgments about figures and cases in human history. Exegetes developed the theory that, in composing the *Annals*, Confucius had donned the mantle of an "uncrowned king." By preserving his "praise and blame" in the *Annals* Confucius had meted out everlasting rewards and punishments to the figures recorded in the text, since they would forever after bear the reputation for good or ill that he had affixed to them.

In carrying out his royal mandate, Confucius had himself adhered to the rule of "sustaining the perishing, reviving the extinct." His worst condemnation was reserved for those who profaned the sacred ancestral prerogatives of the vassal houses by cutting off their line of descent. Moreover, in preserving the memory of houses that had been destroyed, Confucius granted them cultural immortality, thus effectively "reviving the extinct."[79]

All these meanings and implications are invoked in the *Huainanzi*'s deployment of this familiar formula at the opening of "Bing lüe." Upon seeing it, Han-era readers would have immediately called to mind the Masters' texts and exegetical works in which it figured prominently and would have understood that the *Huainanzi* was using "Bing lüe" as a forum in which to discuss particular issues. Indeed, by giving such prominence to this adage, the *Huainanzi* tied "Bing lüe" into a discourse that had been unfolding for several centuries concerning the normatively correct relationship between central and local power.

During the fourth and third centuries B.C.E., when the texts containing the oldest instances of this maxim were likely written, the ideal of "sustaining the perishing, reviving the extinct" was already fast becoming anachronistic. The hereditary, kinship-based institutions on which the Zhou aristocratic order had been founded were giving way to new forms of social and political organization rooted in principles of routinized power and meritocracy. As noted, the hundred-plus vassal states chartered by the Zhou at the dynasty's founding had already been radically reduced in number at the outset of the Warring States, and the process of conglomeration accelerated rapidly as the period unfolded. By the middle of the fourth century B.C.E., seven great kingdoms were virtually the only survivors of the old Zhou order, headed by the last aristocratic houses to have preserved their hereditary positions. Each of these seven kingdoms controlled vast tracts of territory that had at one time been parceled out to dozens of hereditary vassals.

The lone existence of these seven mega-kingdoms thus entailed a radical reorganization of power at the local level. The territory of each kingdom was progressively divided into administrative units known as *jun* (prefectures) and *xian* (districts).[80] These units were not the hereditary bequest of any noble house but were administered by centrally appointed magistrates chosen and assessed on the basis of their expertise in governance. Each magistrate oversaw the collection of taxes, the enforcement of laws, and the administration of public works in his locality for a set period until rotating to another post. The people in most localities thus no longer gave their allegiance to a neighboring lord on the basis of his traditional claims to their fealty but obeyed the official in charge, whoever he was, because of the powers invested in his office by the state.

The history of the Warring States is thus largely that of the competition between these two modes of authority: one traditional and charismatic, the other novel and routine. For the most part, moreover, the competition was one-sided. New routine forms of organization, by virtue of being more stable and yielding more economic and social control for the state, successively displaced traditional hereditary kinship structures through a process of natural selection.

Despite this accelerating trend, however, support for the older Zhou institutions remained strong, especially among the Masters and their disciples, as evinced by the wide promotion of "sustaining the perishing, reviving the extinct" in so many Masters' texts. Some of this support was ideological, idealistic, or merely nostalgic. But in part it was driven by pragmatic concerns. By the late fourth century B.C.E., the seven mega-kingdoms of the Warring States appeared to be in strategic deadlock. It seemed inconceivable that any one kingdom could accumulate sufficient power to destroy the other six. Moreover, even if such a feat were possible, it was unclear that the routine structures that were so successful kingdom by kingdom could be applied comprehensively on the scale of *tian xia* (all under Heaven), the entire civilized world. Magistrates needed to be monitored and disciplined by the central court, and it was questionable whether a single world-spanning court could ever effectively do the job being done by the seven courts of the Warring States.

In that environment, exhortations to "sustain the perishing, revive the extinct" constituted a plea for a political (as opposed to a totally military) settlement to the geostrategic conflict of the Warring States. Advocates of this position were urging the leaders of the day to accept that absolute victory was neither possible nor practical. Total central-ization of *tian xia* neither could be achieved nor could work if it were; thus the new order that replaced the Zhou would have to preserve, at least in part, the sacred sacrificial prerogatives of some few aristocratic houses. One royal house of the Warring States would ascend to be-come the new Son of Heaven, and the remaining royal houses would persist as regional vassals of that new supreme overlord.

Even after the conquest of his six rival kingdoms by the First Em-peror of Qin in 221 B.C.E. belied the notion that total victory was im-possible, the notion of "sustaining the perishing, reviving the extinct" was not immediately discredited or abandoned. The religious mys-tique of the ancestral cult remained strong, and a debate ensued at the Qin court as to whether the Qin house should divide the realm among hereditary vassals in emulation of the Zhou. Only after forceful argu-ments were put forward by Counselor in Chief Li Si (d. 208 B.C.E.) did the First Emperor settle on a policy of total centralization and lo-cal routinization for his newly conquered empire, dividing the entire realm into prefectures and districts.[81]

With the complete collapse of the Qin empire in the wake of the First Emperor's death, the question of "sustaining the perishing, reviv-ing the extinct" became open again. The failure of Qin discredited the radically centralized policies of that dynasty; thus as Liu Bang, the founding ruler of the Han dynasty, laid out the organization of his new empire, he was inclined to look favorably on hereditary kinship struc-tures established on the Zhou model. The Han founder embraced a hybrid system of rule combining the new centralized forms of the Qin and the traditional Zhou institutions of vassalage. An imperial domain surrounding the capital of Chang'an in the west was divided into cen-trally controlled prefectures and districts. In the regions to the east, constituting two-thirds of its territory, the empire was divided up into ten vassal kingdoms ruled by Liu Bang's loyal lieutenants, sons, and brothers.[82]

Almost immediately, the institutions of vassalage became prob-lematic for the Han. Liu Bang became increasingly suspicious of the power of the vassal kings who were not his own kin. One by one, most often violently, they were eliminated and replaced with members of the Liu clan, until by 196 B.C.E., less than a decade after the founding of the dynasty, no vassal kings remained who were not the emperor's blood kin. Even then the hybrid system established by the Han founder remained prone to instability. Persistent friction existed between the Liu kings and the central court, occasionally breaking out into open rebellion or civil war. Inevitably, the central court embarked on a program of consolidation. Successive steps were taken to reduce the size and power of the vassal kingdoms, progressively arrogating the resources and territory of the empire to the control of the central court and curtailing the freedom and independence of the vassal kings.

Liu An and his family were deeply enmeshed in this conflict. The kingdom of Huainan was created in 203 B.C.E. and initially granted to Ying Bu, a non-kin ally of Liu An's grandfather, the Han founder, Liu Bang. Ying Bu rebelled unsuccessfully against the central court in 196, and after his death his kingdom was granted to Liu An's father, Liu Chang. As Liu Bang's son, Liu Chang evidently felt well placed to succeed his father as emperor, but he was passed over in the line of succession in favor of two brothers, known posthumously as Emperor Hui and Emperor Wen. Liu Chang resented being snubbed in this fashion and rebelled against his brother Emperor Wen in 174 B.C.E. His rebellion was put down, and he was sentenced to exile but died while being moved under guard.

The kingdom of Huainan was thus temporarily abolished, converted into centrally controlled administrative districts. In 164 B.C.E., this policy was reversed, though with some adjustments. The very large kingdom of Huainan was divided into three smaller vassalages: Huainan, Hengshan, and Lujiang, each of which was granted to one of Liu Chang's surviving sons. As the eldest brother, Liu An succeeded to his father's title but in a domain much diminished from its former glory.[83]

From this purchase, Liu An was undoubtedly acutely aware of the persistent friction between the court and the vassal kingdoms, and of the general trend in the empire toward increased consolidation of central control. The grand summa that he sponsored thus speaks directly to this issue, and in ways that unsurprisingly (though not unreasoningly) favor the perspective of a vassal king. Although passages relevant to this question can be found throughout the *Huainanzi*, "Bing lüe" presented a natural and uniquely opportune forum in which to devote focused and intensive discussion to the issue.

Why would this be the case? In fact, the military was a principal institutional "crucible" in which new forms of organization and authority had been developed over the course of the late Zhou dynasty, and the military literature of the Warring States was one of the first discursive forums in which the nature and implications of these new structures were articulated and explored. Because military conflicts became increasingly high stakes early on, it was in the military arena that Chinese leaders first experimented with promotion by merit, discrete division of labor, absolute centralization of control, and chains of command grounded in the routine authority of offices rather than the charismatic authority of individuals.

As the application of these concepts became more pervasive and normalized, military organizations (that is, armies) progressively resembled the aristocratic social and political world less and less. Where high position was based on birth in the aristocratic world, it was based on knowledge and experience in the army. Where high-level aristocrats had to operate in a spirit of deference to the prerogatives of their aristocratic underlings, the army enforced an ethos of absolute conformity and unified discipline; as the *Sunzi* said, the skilled commander should be able to maneuver the entire army as if it were a single person.[84] Where tasks were attended to among the aristocracy on an ad hoc basis, in the army responsibilities were strictly divided and individual accountability was enforced.

The success of these new practices in the military arena inspired their broader application to other dimensions of state power. Intensifying competition awoke Chinese leaders to the fact that the contest between states was not merely military but economic, diplomatic, and political as well. States thus could and did gain a competitive edge by enforcing meritocracy, command discipline, and division of labor among their civil functionaries. As these concepts were brought over and applied in the realm of court and local governance, it was done in self-conscious awareness that such restructuring entailed the "militarization" of the political realm. When the First Emperor converted the entire civilized world into prefectures and districts, for example, that was an explicit militarization of the empire.

The military chapter was thus inevitably a venue in which Liu An would choose to address the tensions surrounding his position and that of the kingdom of Huainan in the Han imperial enterprise. His own title of king harkened back to the older kinship model of the Zhou. He thus faced the choice of rejecting the new culture reflected in the military corpus or finding a way of reconciling his own status with the organizational logic of an increasingly militarized world. We have seen that "Bing lüe" fits organically into the tradition of military letters reaching back to the *Sunzi bingfa*, so Liu An and his clients clearly did not choose the former option. They adopted a strategy of reconciliation, and their foregrounding of the principle of "sustaining the perishing, reviving the extinct" was its centerpiece.

After establishing the sacrosanct and inviolate nature of the prerogatives of the hereditary vassal houses with its opening lines, "Bing lüe" sustains and elaborates on this concept over the entire course of the text. In section 15.2, the text incorporates material describing the political dimension of a successful campaign. As a hegemon or king approaches the suburbs of an opponent's capital, he must first issue instructions to the army:

> "Do not cut down trees;
>   do not disturb graves;
>   do not scorch the five grains;
>   do not burn property;
>   do not take the people as slaves;
>   do not steal the six domestic animals."

He then issues a series of proclamations:

> . . . "The ruler of X kingdom has scorned Heaven and insulted the ghosts.
>   He has imprisoned the innocent;
>   he has wrongfully executed the blameless.

This is what is punished by Heaven,
what is hated by the people.
The coming of the military is to cast aside the unrighteous and to restore the virtuous. Anyone who opposes the Way of Heaven and leads
those who rob the people will be killed and his clan exterminated.

Anyone who leads his family to obey will be given an income
for his household;
anyone who leads his village to obey will be rewarded with
[control of] his village;
anyone who leads his town to obey will be given his town as a
fief.
Anyone who leads his district to obey will be made marquis of
his district."

The politics of victory here are completely in line with the dic-
tates of "sustaining the perishing, reviving the extinct." The mission
of the military is founded entirely on ethical grounds; it is not driven
by economic or geostrategic motives as the *Sunzi bingfa* would advo-
cate. The resolution of the campaign results in no material profit for
the victor. The victorious ruler does not arrogate the resources of the
vanquished state to himself through the creation of centrally administered prefectures and districts; rather, he returns all its assets back
to its people in the form of newly created vassalages bequeathed in
exchange for submission. He forbids his army to destroy the enemy's
wealth, not so that he can use it for himself but so that the conquered
state will continue to be able to serve its people and its spirits in the
wake of the campaign.

In the conclusion of section 15.2, "Bing lüe" notes that these constraints are as much pragmatic as they are ethical. If the people of a
state are being tormented by a cruel ruler and can count on magnani-
mous treatment from the invading sovereign, they "yearn for the [in-
vading] military [just] as they hope for rain during a drought or plead
for water when they are thirsty. Who among them will lift a weapon to
meet the [invading] military?" Under such circumstances, a sovereign
can hope to "conclude without battle," which is "the ultimate of the
righteous military." Here "Bing lüe" appropriates and reworks a famil-

iar trope from the *Sunzi bingfa*. In the *Sunzi*, the commander achieves the "ultimate" of victory without battle through clever planning and deception; in the *Huainanzi*, however, it is achieved through adherence to the ideal of "sustaining the perishing, reviving the extinct."

This break from the perspective of the *Sunzi bingfa* is quite pronounced and is in part explicable by the strategic context assumed by the text. The scene described here is a campaign launched by a "hegemon or king," and thus it is not a contest between two peers (as is generally assumed to be the case in the *Sunzi bingfa*) but a punitive expedition launched by a lord against his own vassal. This literary context is uniquely suited to the conditions of the imperial age, but the shift in perspective it represents is not reducible to a mere shift in historical circumstances.

This entire section of "Bing lüe" closely parallels text found in the *Lüshi chunqiu*,[85] the text written under the patronage of the Qin prime minister Lü Buwei *prior to* Qin's unification of the empire. In that earlier text, this scene would have read in the subjunctive, as a description of a sovereign who *would become* hegemon or king (by implication, the ruler of Qin). In that sense, this material broadcast the possibility of a politically achieved unification: Qin was prepared to honor the hereditary privileges of its rival states if they would submit to vassalage under a new Qin dynasty. That was only one position among many, however, from which the *Huainanzi* was free to choose in adapting the military literature of the classical era (a position, moreover, that Qin itself ultimately repudiated). Other texts advocated total abrogation of the hereditary position of the vanquished and the conversion of the conquered territory to centralized, bureaucratic control: "When the sage attacks and annexes another's state he tears down their walls, burns their bells and drums, disperses their stores, scatters their sons and daughters, divides their territory in investing the able; this is known as 'Heaven's achievement.'"[86] In adapting the material from the *Lüshi chunqiu*, the *Huainanzi* transposed its significance from the subjunctive to the prescriptive, declaring that the military power of the empire must be wielded in due deference to the sacred position of the vassal houses in order to be effective.

There is another dimension in which "sustaining the perishing, reviving the extinct" represents a pragmatic as well as an ethical constraint on the use of military force. "Bing lüe" acknowledges that training, discipline, and clever tactics can all achieve effective results, even in the face of the moral and political opposition of the common people. A state and its sacred institutions can be annihilated through terror and violence, but such conquests are not sustainable for the victor. This is because such deeds defy not only human sentiment but also the deep structural patterns of the cosmos itself. The chapter concludes with a warning: if a campaign is launched against a state that is not "without the Way" (that is, one not ruled by a tyrant), various calamities will befall the aggressor through the mechanism of cosmic resonance: people will fall ill, the harvest will perish, the winds and rains will come out of season, the commander will die early (15.26).[87] Military success thus hinges on accordance with the ethos of "sustaining the perishing, reviving the extinct."

"Bing lüe" does not posit these concepts as empty assertions but offers historical precedent in support of its contentions. In section 15.8, the reader is presented with two historical examples. The first is the kingdom of Chu, a southern power that grew to enormous size during the Warring States through the conquest of its neighbors.[88] Despite having vast and easily defensible territory, abundant resources, and a huge population, Chu went down to cataclysmic defeat. The second example offered by section 15.8 is the direct predecessor of the Han dynasty, the Second Emperor of Qin: "Nowhere that human footprints reached or that was traversed by boat and oar was not his prefecture or district." Despite having central control of the entire world, his empire proved unsustainable; the collapse of Qin after less than two decades of rule was set in motion by the rebellion of a minor official, Chen Sheng.[89]

The examples of Chu and Qin present two lessons, from the perspective of the *Huainanzi*. The first is that the new types of military and political mobilization and organization developed in the Warring States had genuine strategic power. The *Huainanzi* does not present an argument for political primitivism. Directly before its discussion of Chu and Qin, in section 15.7, "Bing lüe" presents a model of the ideally rational military structure, enumerating the five offices established in a "modern" army and describing in detail the discrete duties of each. This discussion ends with a celebration of central control:

> These five officers are to the commander as the arms, legs, hands, and feet are to the body. He must choose men, assess their talents, [and] make sure that [each] officer can shoulder his responsibilities [and each] man is capable of his task.
> He instructs them with regulations;
> he applies them with orders;
> using them the way that
> tigers and leopards use their claws and teeth;
> flying birds use their wings.

This is the antithesis of the ethos of the Zhou-era aristocracy. No noble would submit to being manipulated as an instrument in this fashion, and obligations of kinship and status would preclude an aristocratic leader from interacting with his subordinates in this unequivocally authoritative manner. Despite defending the sacred position of the vassal houses, the *Huainanzi* does not call for a return to the days of aristocratic privilege and chivalric protocol. The world has moved on, and the institutes of aristocracy have proved less efficient and effective than the new, more rational structures of recent provenance. In latter days, the bureaucratization of the functional organs of state (including but not limited to the military) must be the norm.

At the same time that the initial success of Chu and Qin demonstrates the efficiency and necessity of these new political forms, however, the ultimate failure of Chu and Qin evinces their natural limits. Superior discipline and organization will give a state a competitive advantage in the short term, but reliance on such assets is, in the conceptual terms of the *Huainanzi*, to depend on the branches and to abandon the root. The sacrosanct sovereignty of the regional states is the root on which all military power is founded, and thus any strategy that exceeds those organic constraints will become self-subverting:

The territory of Tang [the founder of the Shang dynasty] was
seventy *li* square, and he became king. This was because he
cultivated his Moral Potency.

Earl Zhi had a thousand *li* of land and perished. This was because he was exclusively martial.

Thus, [the ruler of]
a thousand-chariot state that practices civility and Potency will
become king;
a ten-thousand-chariot state that is fond of using the military
will perish. (15.9)

By presenting the two models of hereditary vassalage and bureaucratized polity in tension with each other, the *Huainanzi* addresses the
question of scale. A routinized power structure will operate effectively
only if there is a proximal sovereign authority that monitors and regu-
lates its conduct in the public interest. This principle precludes the
entire empire being consolidated under the control of a single monarch: the regulatory function of the sovereign is not practicable on that
scale. Not only does history demonstrate that such large monarchi-
cal domains are unsustainable, moreover, but such structures defy the
guiding parameters of cosmic evolution. From a monistic root, the cosmos naturally developed myriad distinct branches; thus in latter days,
an optimally effective polity should manifest the same fractal pattern.

In that vein, the Han had, according to the *Huainanzi*, instituted
a political structure that perfectly channeled the trajectory of cosmic
evolution. The Han founder, Liu Bang, had reinstated the principle of
"sustaining the perishing, reviving the extinct" by dividing the centralized Qin realm into vassalages ruled by his own kin. In so doing, he established a structure that organically mirrored the root–branches pattern of the cosmos entire: the branches of the regional kings projecting
from the root of the central imperial lineage. Common descent from
the High Ancestor, Liu Bang, tied this entire complex edifice together
into a "Grand Unity."[90]

"Bing lüe" presents an extended defense of the organic necessity of
that political compact. The imperial throne can and should mobilize
military forces organized according to the novel principles laid down

in texts like the *Sunzi bingfa*, but if the dynasty is to survive, those assets must be employed in absolute deference to the hereditary sovereignty of the branch vassalages of the Liu clan like that of Huainan. Total militarization of the Han empire is anathema; such a policy would send the Han down the same self-destructive path followed by Chu and Qin.

"Bing lüe" is distinctive among the component chapters of the *Huainanzi* in that we are possessed of historical records demonstrating the manner in which Liu An applied its theoretical principles in practice. Four years after presenting him with the *Huainanzi*, Liu An wrote his cousin Emperor Wu a memorial opposing a planned invasion of the territory of Min-Yue, in what is today southeastern China.[91] The region at that time was populated by non-Chinese-speaking people and was divided among a number of petty warlords engaged in persistent internecine conflict. An invasion was planned on the pretext of pacifying the region, but Liu An insisted that such a plan ran counter to the principles of "sustaining the perishing, reviving the extinct."

Liu An's memorial spends much space demonstrating the folly of trying to annex Min-Yue, in the manner of the Qin, as a territory under the central control of the imperial throne. The difficulty of conquering and subduing the territory makes it impossible to convert it into prefectures and districts. Even if one were inclined to use the military according to the profit-driven principles articulated by the *Sunzi bingfa*, this would not be workable, since the losses of such a campaign would far outstrip the gains, thus violating the *Sunzi*'s cardinal rule of strategy.

The moral justification of pacification is likewise abnegated, according to Liu An, by the doctrine of "sustaining the perishing, reviving the extinct." The people of Min-Yue have never paid tribute or made any sign of fealty to the Han throne, and thus they are not vassals. Since the sovereign responsibilities and prerogative of no vassal state are at issue, there is no pretext for sending the military in to redress the situation:

> Thus you should revive their extinct lineage, sustain their perished state, establish them as a regal vassal so as to nurture Yue. At this they

will certainly submit hostages to serve as officers and present tribute regularly. [In this way] Your Majesty, with only a seal one inch square and sash two feet long, will pacify the frontier and spread your awesome virtue, without belaboring a single soldier or blunting a single spear.[92]

What Liu An proposes in this missive as the optimal solution is unsurprising, given the ideas outlined by him earlier in "Bing lüe." As Edmund Ryden notes, the considerations at play in this instance were partly pragmatic, as a full-scale invasion of Min-Yue would have sent large imperial forces through the territory of Huainan, impinging on Liu An's independence (if only temporarily).[93] But it was for similar motives that the *Huainanzi* initially advocated "sustaining the perishing, reviving the extinct" as a general principle for military planning. Here Liu An the vassal applies the same argument to the particular case of Yue that "the Master of Huainan" made in the abstract in his eponymous text: all military power must be built on the foundation established by the sovereign hereditary lineages into which the world is divided, *not* vice versa.

"Bing lüe" closes with a ritual scene that ingeniously illustrates and reinforces this principle. Presumably drawing from a now-lost text,[94] section 15.26 outlines the protocol that is to be followed when a military commander is commissioned with the execution of a campaign. The ruler and the commander convene in the Great Temple for the ceremony of investiture. The ruler presents the commander with the symbolic *yue* ax, insignia of his authority, and intones, "From here up to Heaven is controlled by [you,] the commander." He repeats a variant of this formula on presenting the commander with the other part of his insignia, the *fu* ax: "From here down to the Abyss is controlled by [you,] the commander." The commander receives these regalia with a ritual response:

> "[Just as] the kingdom cannot be governed from without,
> the army cannot be ruled from within [the court].
> [Just as] one cannot serve the ruler with two minds,
> one cannot respond to the enemy with a doubtful will.

Since [I], your minister, have received control from you, I exclusively [wield] the authority of the drums, flags, and *fu* and *yue* axes. I ask nothing in return. I [only] hope that Your Highness likewise will not hand down one word of command to me.

If Your Highness does not agree, I dare not take command.

If Your Highness agrees, I will take my leave and set out."

The import of these ceremonial formulas is clear: in initiating a military campaign, the ruler temporarily bestows royal authority on the commander charged with its execution. As section 15.26 goes on to describe, the regal powers granted to the commander are total. In the wake of victory, the commander "sets aside land and apportions it, making sure it is outside the feudal mound."[95] The land thus apportioned is to be granted as vassalages in reward for participation in the campaign. In creating new vassals in this way, the commander is literally acting as a pro tempore king. But in accordance with the principles established in section 15.2, this assumption of royal power is unavoidable. Winning the people's compliance through adherence to the rule of "sustaining the perishing, reviving the extinct" is the necessary condition for victory; thus in order to successfully achieve the object of the campaign, the commander must hold regal powers of investiture.

This resolution of "Bing lüe" is highly polemical, and its cogency derives from its basic fidelity to the logic of the military textual tradition. Although the entire scene is cloaked in archaic symbolism and ritual, it basically reiterates a concept posited in the *Sunzi bingfa*: "There are orders from the ruler that [the commander] does not accept."[96] In other words, the military realm is so driven by autonomous imperatives, and its function is so urgent, that it must not be trespassed upon by any outside interference, even from the ruler himself.

"Bing lüe" does not distort this principle in any way but merely pursues it to its logical end: given the intrinsic nature of the military and how it operates, whenever a ruler launches an offensive against another duly constituted lord, he diminishes not only the sovereignty of his opponent but also *his own sovereignty*. The ruler must relinquish his own authority to the commander in order to establish a military force capable of carrying out its mission. In ordering the destruction of another dynast, he is thus potentially inviting his own destruction: the perils of launching a military response to a threat are almost as dire as the peril posed by the threat itself. The use of coercive power in a functional empire can thus never be anything but an extreme emergency measure. The highly efficient military organization envisioned by texts like the *Sunzi bingfa* exists in tension with all forms of charismatic, hereditary authority, including that of the ruler himself. The only check on the danger such an institution poses within a dynastic system is thus an absolute reverence for the principle of "sustaining the perishing, reviving the extinct."

This point is repeatedly underscored in the conclusion to "Bing lüe." It is the basis of the commander's exclusion of land within "the feudal mound," where the ancestral temples of the defeated lord are located, from the bequests dispensed as rewards in the wake of the victorious campaign. Whatever the final disposition of the defeated state, the ancestral cult of its original rulers must be able to continue.[97] If the commander were granted the power to destroy even one hereditary lineage, what could guarantee that the destruction would stop there and would not rebound on the lineage of the commander's own ruler?

The principle is again reinforced in the depiction in "Bing lüe" of the victorious general's return:

> Turning back, he returns to the kingdom, lowering his banners and storing the *fu* and *yue* axes. He makes his final report to the ruler, saying, "I have no further control over the army." He then dons coarse silk and enters seclusion.
>
> [The commander goes] to ask pardon of the ruler. The ruler says, "Spare him." [The commander] withdraws and dons fasting garb. For a great victory, he remains secluded for three years; for a middling victory, two years; for a lesser victory, one year.

Despite his success and the wickedness of the enemy ruler, the returning commander must ask his own ruler's pardon and do penance for his actions. His "crime" is twofold. First, he has committed lèse-majesté in assuming royal powers on campaign. Second, he has violated the sacred prerogatives of a duly constituted vassal lineage. In the Han system, this second offense would be compounded by the fact that in attacking a vassal, the commander had done violence to the ruler's own paternal kin.

The seeming incongruousness of this scene is very deliberate; it is deployed to illustrate the inherently transgressive nature of a meritocratic, bureaucratic military operating within a dynastic polity. Emperors may relish the power that a professionalized military apparatus puts at their disposal, but unless they would undermine the very logic on which their own position rests, they must insist that the military function within the constraints of the ethos of "sustaining the perishing, reviving the extinct." The organic homeostasis that must persist for the throne and the military to coexist thus, within the theoretical world of the *Huainanzi*, makes the position of Liu An and his court of Huainan sacrosanct.

Spiritlike 神 and Enlightened 明: "Bing lüe" and Daoism

It may come as a surprise to many general readers that the question of the existence of Daoism during the Former Han dynasty is a very vexed one in European and American scholarship.[98] A Daoist church claims millions of adherents today and has existed for more than two millennia, but its historical origins are murky and much contested. Although two Warring States texts, the *Laozi* and the *Zhuangzi*, are conventionally cited as the "founding" texts of Daoism, there is no evidence that they were treated as such at the time of their composition. As early as the Warring States, the latter-day disciples of Confucius, for example, identified themselves and were identified by others as Ru, but there is no mention of a "Daoist" tradition or Daoist adherents until the second century B.C.E., when the term first appeared in an essay by the historian Sima Tan (d. 110 B.C.E.).[99]

Even if the existence of Daoism could be confidently established, the question of the *Huainanzi*'s affiliation with a Daoist tradition is likewise very complex. Given the eclectic nature of its contents, early

Chinese bibliographers declared it a *za*, or "miscellaneous" text.[100] Modern interpreters should not be bound by this classification, but deeming it a "Daoist" text is problematic if we turn to the claims of the text itself, which are far more dispositive on the issue than the judgment of imperial bibliographers. The *Huainanzi* insists that it is bound by no one tradition but combines all the different forms of knowledge and inquiry in the world into a single, perfect synthesis. Thus to say that it belonged to one "Daoist" tradition among many competing systems of thought is to refute the claims that the text makes about itself.[101]

Acknowledging the intractability of the problem does not settle the issue, however. I do not intend to tackle the question of Daoism's origins or the "correct" filiation of the *Huainanzi*, which are beyond the scope of this study. To do so would in any case be irrelevant to an exploration of the relationship of "Bing lüe" to Daoism. Simply asking whether "Bing lüe" (or any other part of the *Huainanzi*) is Daoist is far too simplistic an approach to the historical forces at work in the production and use of the text. Although the evidence about the status of Daoism is ambiguous and open to differing interpretations, the textual record gives a clear account of debates transpiring during the Former Han of which the *Huainanzi* was a part. These debates were not isolated to the time of the *Huainanzi* but had earlier implicated Warring States texts such as the *Laozi* and *Zhuangzi* and continued down to the time of the founding of the Daoist church in 184 C.E. It is thus only by situating "Bing lüe" (and the *Huainanzi* as a whole) in these ongoing debates that its relationship to the history of Daoism can be meaningfully explored, and this is what I intend to do in the following pages. In brief, I hope to demonstrate how certain positions that the *Huainanzi* took in debates of the Former Han developed arguments put forward in earlier texts such as the *Laozi* and *Zhuangzi* and set the groundwork for positions taken by later founders of the Daoist church. Whether or not the *Huainanzi* was, in any essential sense, a "Daoist" text, by playing the role that it did in the intellectual milieu of its time, it materially contributed to the historical processes that gave us the Daoist church of today.

A prime example of a debate that the *Huainanzi* engaged very intensely was that surrounding the issue of personal cultivation. From the earliest days of the Warring States, various thinkers had differed over the question of personal cultivation's relevance to government. Some Masters contended that, since the quality of a government was a product of the quality of its officials, the state had to take an active role in guiding the development of its officials' characters.[102] Other Masters contended that people did not vary so widely in character or that, if they did, their characters were not subject to change or improvement.[103] From this perspective, the state did not have to concern itself with the personal cultivation of its officials. It had only to construct the right kinds of institutions and establish the right kind of rules, so that the bad aspects of human character would be suppressed and the useful aspects harnessed.

In this general argument, which has continued in various forms for all of Chinese history (and continues even today), the *Huainanzi* came down squarely on the side of the urgency of personal cultivation for the state and its leaders. For example, in chapter 9 ("The Ruler's Techniques"), section 8, we read,

> During the reign of King Tang [of the Shang dynasty], there was a seven-year drought. The king offered himself as sacrifice at Mulberry Forest. Thereupon
> > clouds from the Four Seas gathered,
> > and rain fell for a thousand *li*.
> Embracing his basic substance and imparting his sincerity, he evoked a response from Heaven and Earth, his spirit making itself known beyond the [four] quarters. How could promulgating orders and prohibitions suffice to accomplish something like this?
> In ancient times, the Utmost Essence of the sage-kings took form within themselves, and their personal likes and dislikes were forgotten outside themselves. They
> > spoke simply to express their emotions,
> > issued orders to make clear their intentions,
> > displayed [their essential qualities] in rites and music,
> > and exemplified them in songs and ballads.
> Their achievements
> > have spread to a myriad generations without being impeded

and have pervaded the four directions without being depleted. Even birds, beasts, and insects were refined and transformed by them. How much more so were they effective in maintaining laws and carrying out commands. Thus,

> the loftiest [of rulers] transforms by means of his spirit.
> The next lower [ruler] convinces the people to act without transgressions.
> The next lower one rewards the worthy and punishes the unruly.[104]

This passage is one of many in the *Huainanzi* that lays out the essential relationship between governance and personal cultivation. Performing the correct action or applying the correct rule is key in any given instance (such as Tang's performance of the ritual at Mulberry Forest), but even more essential to the success of any endeavor is *being* the right kind of person. Tang could not have evoked a response from Heaven and Earth if he had not beforehand developed the "basic substance" and "sincerity" activated by his sacrifice.

The *Huainanzi* is quite unequivocal in its assertion of the potential power of personal cultivation. This is implied by the quoted passage in the idea of "transformation by the spirit." The "spirit" here is not an abstract quality of personality but the matrix of animating energy (*qi*) suffusing the mind and body that is the basis of consciousness and vitality.[105] The notion here is that the most excellent ruler can have a harmonizing effect on those around him without doing or saying anything, merely by radiating beneficent energy from the core of his being. This is why the influence of such "transformation" is effective even on birds, beasts, and insects: it operates at a purely material level, independent of human institutions, culture, or even language. Not everyone is capable of such "spirit transformation"; it can be achieved only by one who has refined his or her mind and body through rigorous cultivation. The text does not deny that mechanisms like laws, commands, rewards, and punishments can and do produce effective results, but it does insist that such measures will not sustain a harmonious polity in the long term unless they are undertaken by leaders who embody, to at least some degree, the qualities of personal excellence that make spirit transformation possible.

This position put the *Huainanzi* on one distinct side of a polemical divide running through the political culture of the Former Han. If the textual record is to be believed, many servitors of the Han government scoffed at the notion that personal cultivation was of any concern to the state.[106] Even if some cultivation were necessary before one could serve in government, that was the private affair of individuals *before* taking office. The government did not have to concern itself with how people prepared themselves to serve; it had only to set up rules and institutions that would efficiently recruit the able and incentivize them to work to their maximum potential. The *Huainanzi* held that such ideas were folly: the abandonment of the root in favor of the branch.

Advocating the importance of personal cultivation did not, in and of itself, situate the *Huainanzi* within the long history of Daoism. There were many advocates of personal cultivation before, during, and after the Former Han who would never have represented themselves or have been identified by others, even posthumously, as Daoist. The most significant group in this regard were the Ru, or latter-day followers of Confucius. For Confucians, personal cultivation was of paramount importance: an individual could not be of any use as a leader unless he had developed qualities of excellence that made him fit to serve.

Comparison of the *Huainanzi* with earlier and contemporary Confucian texts, however, reveals deep divisions among Former Han advocates of personal cultivation. The *Huainanzi* disagreed with Confucians as to both the goals and the methods of personal cultivation. For Confucians, the chief mode of cultivation was learning (*xue*). Learning could take on many forms: participation in ritual, discussion with friends and teachers, even interaction with family members. Central to any course of learning was the study of texts, however, especially the writings of Confucius and the ancient sage-kings. Through immersion in this program of learning, which brought the student into contact with an ever-widening array of people in antiquity and the current day, an individual would develop moral qualities such as Humaneness and Rightness, becoming overall a *junzi*, or Superior Man.[107]

By contrast, the *Huainanzi*'s prescriptions denigrated learning, especially textual study, as an inferior form of attainment. It advocated an array of goals and practices very different from those embraced by Confucians in their pursuit of moral perfection:

> Shallow scholars in this declining age do not understand how to get to the origins of their minds and return to their root. They merely sculpt and polish their natures and adorn and stifle their genuine responses in order to interact with their age. Thus,
>> when their eyes desire something, they forbid it with measures;
>> when their minds delight in something, they restrict it with rites.
>
> They hasten forth in circles and formally scrape and bow
>> while the meat goes bad and becomes inedible
>> and the wine goes sour and becomes undrinkable.
>> Externally they restrict their bodies;
>> internally they belabor their minds.
>> They damage the harmony of yin and yang
>> and constrain the genuine responses of their nature to fate.
>
> Thus throughout their lives, they are sorrowful people.
>> Those who penetrate through to the Way are not like this.
>> They regulate the genuine responses of their natures,
>> cultivate the techniques of the mind,
>> nourish these with harmony,
>> take hold of these through suitability.
>> They delight in the Way and forget what is lowly;
>> They find repose in Potency and forget what is base.
>> Since their natures desire nothing, they attain whatever they desire.
>> Since their minds delight in nothing, there are no delights in which they do not partake.
>> Those who do not exceed their genuine responses do not allow them to tie down their Potency.
>> Those who find ease in their natures do not allow them to injure their inner harmony.

Thus with
>   their relaxed bodies, their untrammeled awareness,
>   their standards and regulations,
> they can become models for the empire.[108]

Where Confucians found ultimate value in the culture created by sages of high antiquity, the *Huainanzi* (following earlier texts like the *Laozi* and *Zhuangzi*) advocated that the adept "penetrate through to the Way" that precedes human culture and human morality, even human beings themselves. In its formulations, the power of institutions such as ritual and values such as Humaneness and Rightness is vastly surpassed by that of the root that can be accessed by delving into one's own nature. Because this root is common to all things, accessing it does not require interaction with other people:

> The essentials of the world:
>   do not lie in the Other
>   but instead lie in the self;
>   do not lie in other people
>   but instead lie in your own person.
> When you fully realize it [the Way] in your own person, then all the myriad things will be arrayed before you. When you thoroughly penetrate the teachings of the Techniques of the Mind, then you will be able to put lusts and desires, likes and dislikes, outside yourself.[109]

The mention of "Techniques of the Mind" here points to one of the key differences between the program of personal cultivation advocated in the *Huainanzi* and the path of learning exalted by Confucians. The patron and authors of the *Huainanzi* were obviously literati, and they acknowledged that literacy and erudition were necessary attributes of a leader in latter days. They insisted contra the Confucians, however, that textual learning is not a path toward the realization of the human being's highest potential. In order to achieve the *Huainanzi*'s ideal of being a Genuine Person or one of the Perfected,[110] one had to commit to a regimen of apophatic practices aimed at "penetrating through to the Way" in one's own person. The *Huainanzi* does not give explicit instructions for the performance of these practices, but many passages in the text make clear the types of regimens that are involved:

> To block off the nine orifices,
> to store up the attention of the mind,
> to discard hearing and vision,
> to return to having no awareness,
> to vastly wander outside the dust and dirt and freely roam in the activity of effortlessness, to inhale the yin and exhale the yang, and to completely harmonize with the myriad things, this is Potency.[111]

The text is clearly describing a practice of breathing meditation. This is one of the key "Techniques of the Mind" advocated in the *Huainanzi*. The goal of this practice is to quiet the constant stream of thought, feeling, and perception that is the ordinary condition of consciousness, so as to experience the placid stillness of pure "spirit" that is the lodging of the mind and the latent baseline of awareness. At that point, consciousness is wholly merged with the Way and free of all bias, misconception, and delusion; thus the practitioner can unlock the full potential of the cosmic origin through delving deeply into his or her own being.

Other practices advocated in the text include yogic exercise and dietary regimen. This total focus on both mind and body is in keeping with the *Huainanzi*'s concept of the Way and its relationship to the individual. The presence of the Way in the person is not purely metaphysical; it is lodged in the *qi* that composes one's flesh, blood, organs, mind, and spirit. The more suffused one's mind and body are with the dynamic, undifferentiated *qi* like that of the cosmic origin (called Quintessential Spirit in the text), the more clearly one will embody the Way in consciousness and action. Because the mind and body are part of a single continuous system for the circulation and refinement of *qi*, any program aimed at embodying the Way must necessarily include physical activities as well as contemplative practices.

In the root–branches scheme of the *Huainanzi* as a whole, this program of apophatic personal cultivation is the root of the imperial enterprise. In the age of "Utmost Potency" at the beginning of time, "the sages [merely] inhaled and exhaled the *qi* of yin and yang, and none of the myriad living things failed to flourish."[112] In other words, in the beginning rulers could maintain good order merely through attention to their own personal cultivation. In latter days, government requires a complex array of skills and techniques, but all good order yet begins with rulers and ministers who are dedicated to perfecting themselves through practices like the "Techniques of the Mind."

The advocacy of this body of practice links the *Huainanzi* to earlier texts on which it drew and to later texts foundational to the Daoist church. Debates over the nature of personal cultivation had been ongoing since the Warring States. Like the *Huainanzi*, the *Laozi*, the *Zhuangzi*, and other early texts such as the *Nei ye* promoted the refinement of the mind and body through meditation, yoga, and dietary regimen in explicit contradiction of the Confucian advocacy of learning. Many of these practices later became central to the spiritual life of Daoist communities in the Later Han and beyond.[113]

Understanding the nature and goals of these personal cultivation practices is essential to understanding the distinctive perspective of military affairs offered in "Bing lüe." The *Huainanzi* insists that the root–branches organization of the phenomenal world is all encompassing. Not only can the cosmos as a whole be analyzed into root and branches, but every component realm of the universe displays the same pattern. Thus military affairs, while being a branch outgrowth of the human condition, still likewise have their own root and branches. As is true for kingship more generally, the root of military command does not lie in any discrete knowledge or skill:

Now everyone in the world
    knows to work at studying its branches,
    and none knows to resolve to cultivate its root.
This is to discard the root and plant the limbs. [15/145/1–8]
    Those things that assist the military in victory are many; those that ensure victory are few.
        If armor is sturdy and weapons sharp,
        chariots are solid and horses excellent,

rations and equipment sufficient,
officers and men numerous,
these are the great foundations of the army, yet victory is not [found]
here. If one is clear about
the movements of the stars, planets, sun, and moon;
the rules of recision and accretion and the occult arts;
the advantages of the rear, front, left, and right;
these are aids to warfare, yet completeness is not [found] here.
That by which the excellent commander is ensured victory is his
constant possession of a knowledge without origin, a Way that is not
a Way. It is difficult to share with the multitude. (15.6)

The language that "Bing lüe" uses throughout to describe the ideal
commander makes clear that this is a figure perfected through the
same program of personal cultivation advocated earlier in the text for
the ruler and his civil officials. Unless the commander can embody
the Way in the working of his mind and body, he will not have the
capabilities that can ensure victory. In positing these assertions, the
Huainanzi leverages off of basic principles established in the early military literature. If, as the *Sunzi bingfa* and other early texts attest, command is an intellectual enterprise, then it is subject to all the pitfalls
and vulnerabilities that beset the human intellect. The *Sunzi* itself
acknowledges this when it declares that victory depends on the commander's ability to employ the "extraordinary," some unprecedented
and unanticipated maneuver that can subvert the enemy commander,
undermining his efforts to make sense of the tactical situation.[114] This
is fine in theory, but if all commanders are on the lookout for "extraordinary" moves, how can one be assured of effectively executing one?
The answer in "Bing lüe" is that the interplay between "extraordinary"
and "usual" responses is too complex to be completely and reliably
fathomed by the ordinary human mind. It requires the operation of
a consciousness that has been elevated through personal cultivation:

The commander must see singularly and know singularly.
Seeing singularly is to see what is not seen.
Knowing singularly is to know what is not known.

> To see what others do not is called "enlightenment."
> To know what others do not is called "spiritlike."
> The spiritlike and enlightened is one who triumphs in advance. He
> who triumphs in advance
>> cannot be attacked when he defends,
>> cannot be defeated in battle,
>> cannot be defended against when he attacks. (15.25)

"Spiritlike" and "enlightened" are qualities attributed to the Sage and the Genuine Person in earlier chapters of the *Huainanzi*.[115] As discussed earlier, the spirit is the level of consciousness at which awareness is perfectly merged with the Way, thus "spiritlike" perception is all encompassing and totally comprehensive: one sees the situation from the perspective of the all-pervading Way, with perfect clarity and detachment. Moreover, the benefits of personal cultivation are not only cognitive and subjective; they totally transform the commander's relationship to the phenomenal world:

> There is no spirit nobler than Heaven;
> there is no force more versatile than Earth;
> there is no motion more swift than time;
> there is no resource more advantageous than people.
> These four are the pillars and trunks of the military, yet they must rely
> on the Way to operate because [the Way] can unite their functions.
>> The advantage of terrain overcomes Heaven and time;
>> clever tactics overcome the advantage of terrain;
>> force overcomes people.
> Thus,
>> one who relies on Heaven can be led astray;
>> one who relies on Earth can be trapped;
>> one who relies on time can be pressured;
>> one who relies on people can be fooled.
> Humaneness, courage, trustworthiness, and incorruptibility are the
> most excellent qualities among people. However,
>> the brave can be lured;
>> the humane can be robbed;

the trustworthy are easily cheated;

the incorruptible are easily schemed against.

If the commander of a host has even one of these [flaws], he will be taken captive. Seen from this perspective, it also is clear that victory in arms is produced by the Pattern of the Way, not by the worthiness of human character.

Thus, deer and elk can be seized by snares;

fish and turtle can be taken by nets;

geese and swans can be collected with the dart and line.

Only to the Formless may nothing be done. For this reason, the sage

> lodges in the Sourceless, so his feelings cannot be grasped and observed;

> moves in the Formless, so his formations cannot be attained and traced.

He has no model and no protocol;

he does what is appropriate [for what] arrives;

he has no name and no shape;

he fashions [a new] image for [each] change.

How deep!

How distant!

Through winter and summer,

through spring and fall,

above reaching the highest branch,

below fathoming the deepest depth,

changing and transforming,

never hesitating or halting,

he sets his mind in the Field of Profound Mystery

and lodges his will in the Spring of the Nine Returns.

Though one has acute eyes, who can detect his feelings? (15.17)

The word translated as "feelings" here, *qing*, has a range of meaning not matched by any English word. It includes feelings but also encompasses thoughts and perceptions—any responses of the human being to external stimuli.[116] The person of the cultivated commander embodies the same dynamic responsiveness of the Way; in all his plans and deeds he thus becomes as inscrutable, unpredictable, and irresistibly effective as the Way itself. This is the response of "Bing lüe" to the conundrum raised by the *Sunzi bingfa*'s theoretical pronouncements: an "extraordinary" maneuver can be truly effected only by an extraordinary individual. Common cleverness and deception will not prevail if one is faced with an opponent who has attained a high level of personal cultivation.

The central role that "Bing lüe" ascribes to the apophatic personal cultivation of the commander is the chief factor that situates it in the *longue durée* history of Daoism. Although it is not at all clear that early texts such as the *Laozi* and *Zhuangzi* anticipated the military applications to which the *Huainanzi* deployed practices such as the "Techniques of the Mind" aimed at "attaining the Way," the engagement of "Bing lüe" with this domain gives it an affinity to these texts that it does not share with early military texts such as the *Sunzi bingfa*. The *Sunzi* describes the commander's comprehension and manipulation of the battlefield as "spiritlike,"[117] but this was presented as an ideal at which to aim, one that could replace the aristocratic vision of a heroic, action-oriented warrior. The *Sunzi* offers no concrete program for becoming "spiritlike"; it is a goal that the reader is set to pursue through the practiced operation of ordinary intellectual powers.[118] "Bing lüe," by contrast, follows the *Laozi* and *Zhuangzi* in using the sobriquet "spiritlike" (among others) to denote an extraordinary aspect of the human potential, one that can be accessed through rigorous efforts at self-transformation that put the individual into communication with the very ground of the cosmos.

Its advocacy of personal cultivation links "Bing lüe" to both early texts that contributed to the origins of Daoism and to later foundational texts of the Daoist church. Another debate that influenced the early history of Daoism in which the *Huainanzi* played a role was over the size and scope of the imperial government. Although "Bing lüe" itself does not contain much discussion that is of direct relevance to this debate, the concepts and themes raised by the *Huainanzi*'s discussion of military affairs take on expanded implications when read in the context of this issue. Thus it is worth discussing here.

Because the Han was, in essence, the first enduring united government of the Chinese world, there was no firm precedent as to what should be its institutional shape or its human composition, leaving many open questions in need of resolution. What essential activities should the government encompass? How should it raise its revenue? What type of functionaries should it employ? The array of answers to these questions championed by different groups in the Han state was complex, but in general the field can be divided between advocates of "big government" and those of "small government." "Big government" partisans favored a state that included many functions and services within its ambit, one that raised its revenues from diverse sources and kept a wide variety of types of personnel in its employ. "Small government" partisans insisted that government's functions should be kept to a bare minimum, that its revenue should come from agricultural taxes alone, and that only a small, select cadre of servitors with very particular qualifications should bear the official credentials of the state.

An outstanding instance of the debate is exemplified by the *Yan tie lun*, which purports to record deliberations held at the Han court in 81 B.C.E. between official proponents of the salt and iron monopolies and Confucian critics (identified in the text as "literati" and "worthies"). At one juncture in the discussions, the officials complain that though edicts are periodically issued for the recruitment of literati and worthies, the government has yet to find personnel in this way that can cure the ills of the populace.[119] The Confucians respond that "in the path of the noble man, the Way of action and cessation is invariably narrow."[120] In other words, official calls for the promotion of the learned and the worthy fail because the government is working with criteria for worthiness that are much too broad. The officials object, asking rhetorically, "What narrowness is there in the Way?"[121] To this the Confucians reply,

In the promoting of knights in antiquity, they were chosen in the villages and selected in the hamlets. Only after their talents and abilities were assessed were they given office, only after they proved capable of their task were they given rank and emolument. . . . In this way the worthy were promoted and the unworthy repressed. Today the Way of officialdom is mixed and indiscriminate. The rich buy office with wealth, the brave aim for merit by killing. Traveling acrobats and dancers all come forward to fill in as officials. Accruing merit for many days, some rise as high as chamberlain or grand councilor. They let dangle the green cord [of office] and carried the official seal, grasping the handles of life and death, holding the Mandate of the myriad people.[122]

This rhetorical salvo by the Confucians of 81 B.C.E. expresses a conceptual formulation that ultimately became quite conventional to the ideology of successive imperial regimes but that was still controversial in the Former Han. By issuing the credentials and insignia of imperial office to unfit individuals, complain the Confucians, the Han has profaned the very Mandate on which its claims to sovereignty rest. This notion of the Mandate of Heaven, that in any given era Heaven bestowed its charge on the single worthiest lineage to rule the world, was a venerable theory of the justification for the state, the origins of which extended back to the founding of the Western Zhou.[123] The concept had evolved dramatically over time and was by no means a point of universal consensus in the early imperial era. It did have many champions, however, among Confucian partisans in the Former Han. As the *Chunqiu fanlu* of Dong Zhongshu proclaimed, the Mandate was a sacred charge that came down to the emperor alone and that he shared with those whom he authorized to bear his insignia and wield his seal: "Only the Son of Heaven receives the Mandate from Heaven, the world receives the Mandate from the Son of Heaven."[124] It thus had to be dispensed very selectively, only to those individuals who could bear it with dignity and live up to its moral provisions.

In this way, adherence to the theory of the "Mandate of Heaven" was a key linchpin in the conceptual armory of those who argued in favor of "small government," since it placed discrete limits on the size of the state. No one seriously expected that the Han could engineer a society in which there were no merchants dealing in salt or iron, for example, but Confucians insisted that such individuals should never bear the insignia of office. By narrowing the parameters within which the empire could recruit and credentialize officials, Confucians effectively limited the scope within which the state could arrogate to itself the human and material resources of society at large.

On what side of this debate did the *Huainanzi* fall? The Mandate of Heaven is mentioned in only a few passages in the entire text and is accorded no role in legitimating the imperial order that the *Huainanzi* as a whole articulates. Instead, as we have seen, the text grounds claims to imperial sovereignty in its cosmology of the Way. Imperial sovereignty does not derive from a unique mandate that comes exclusively through and must be dispensed by the emperor. Rather, the government exists in the shape it does because its structural dynamic, patterned on the Way and the universe emergent from it, will produce order equivalent to that of the cosmos as a whole.

Absent from this theory of imperial sovereignty is a clear boundary line between those sharing in the mandate of the "state" and those relegated to the private domain of the "subjects." Since sovereignty derives from the structure of the cosmos itself, it is dispersed throughout the polity in a gradually attenuating pattern mirroring the cosmogonic dynamic of the universe at large. The broad basis of this sovereignty is underscored at many points in the text:

> [The sage] never fails to use things according to their natural qualities.
> Therefore,
>> if you combine the strength [of many] to lift something, there is nothing in which you cannot succeed.
>> If you collect the wisdom of many, there is nothing you cannot accomplish.
>> You can make a deaf person chew sinews [to soften them], but you cannot make him hear.
>> Physical forms [may] have what is incomplete;
>> abilities may have aspects that are limited.
> Thus a particular form belongs in a particular place, and a particular ability addresses a particular task.
>> If one's strength surpasses his burden, lifting it will not be heavy;
>> if one's ability is appropriate to the task, accomplishing it will not be difficult.

When each matter—small or large, long or short—obtains what is appropriate to it, the world will be as one, and no one will have the means to surpass another. The sage makes use of people's various capacities; thus no talent is wasted.[125]

The legitimacy of the imperial state in this formulation does not reside in the ruler's exclusion of the "wrong kind of people" from government but in his ability to incorporate *all* kinds of people, even the *incapable* or the "unworthy," into an enterprise conducive of societal and cosmic order. The *Huainanzi* does not deny that the employment of people of good character in high office is important to fostering order, but it does repeatedly insist that there is no type of person whose particular character or competence completely disqualifies him from being employed in the government at all: "Of all things in the world, none is more poisonous than the *xitu* plant, but an accomplished doctor puts it in his bag and keeps a supply of it, for it is useful in some treatments. Thus, if among the products of the forests and the thickets, there are none that may be ignored, how much more so is this the case with people?"[126]

This message of breadth and inclusiveness, moreover, is self-consciously contrasted in the *Huainanzi* with the more exclusive theory of sovereignty promulgated by Confucians. The opening of chapter 13 notes that in antiquity government produced political order so spontaneously that there was no need even for insignia and costumes to distinguish officials from the governed.[127] Although this pristine state of simplicity could not be maintained in latter eras, the text does note approvingly that during the early career of Liu Bang, the Han founder, "Those who wore sumptuous clothing and wide sashes and who took Confucianism and Mohism as their way were taken as unworthy,"[128] a state of affairs that changed only when the realm was pacified and such civil officials could be effectively employed. The Confucian notion of sovereignty thus does not comprehend the full spectrum within which the state may make timely and beneficial use of human talents.

There were many points on which the authors of the *Huainanzi* differed with the official party in the *Yan tie lun*. On the broader issue of "big government" versus "small government," however, the two perspectives concur: both groups envisioned a government populated by officials with a much broader array of backgrounds and competences than that allowed for in Confucian political theory, and a government composed of many more diverse component parts and agencies. For both Dong Zhongshu and the literati partisans of the *Yan tie lun*, only those individuals refined by the Confucian classics possessed sufficient moral fiber and dignity to hold official insignia without profaning the Mandate of Heaven that such marks symbolized. By contrast, the *Huainanzi* authors and the officials of the *Yan tie lun* adhered to no such scruples about the baseline criteria for official service. For the *Huainanzi*, the sole determinant of whether a person was fit for office was whether he could contribute to the production of order, and since the political order aspired for by the text was an extension of the cosmic order, any denizen of the cosmos could potentially play a constructive role if the position and task were found to suit his or her inherent capacities.

This dimension of the *Huainanzi* links Liu An's intellectual enterprise to the larger history of Daoism. In the years intervening between the destruction of Liu An's court in 122 B.C.E. and the violent emergence of the Daoist church in 184 C.E., the progressive rise of Confucian literati to positions of control over the policy organs of the Han state steadily alienated from the halls of imperial power those scholars who had identified themselves with ideas and practices that fell outside the purview of Confucian pedagogy. Mastery of the Confucian canon eventually became the exclusive criterion for official employment under the Han. Scholars who practiced the meditative and yogic arts revered at Huainan did not disappear, however. They retreated to positions of lesser elite status in the local society of the rural periphery and continued to preserve both the political and personal cultivation traditions advocated in the *Huainanzi*.

One such scholar was Gan Zhongke from Qi (modern Shandong, the later heartland of the Yellow Turbans), who during the reign of Han Chengdi (r. 33–7 B.C.E.) presented a text called the *Classic of Supreme Peace That Embraces the Origin* to the Han court, claiming that it could revive the mandate of the Han and that he had received it from the Genuine Person Chi Jingzi (Master Essence of Red). He was jailed on the accusations of the Confucian scholar Liu Xiang and died in prison before trial. Some disciples of Gan Zhongke brought the text back to court during the reign of Aidi (r. 7–1 B.C.E.) and enjoyed some success at attracting imperial favor, but they ultimately met the same fate as Gan.[129] Such figures were what the increasingly Confucianized officialdom of the Han deemed *fang shi* 方士, "occult" or "technical" scholars specializing in petty or heterodox arts, whose training did not qualify them for the dignity of imperial office.[130] These men had everything to gain from an imperial polity reimagined along the conceptual lines laid down in the *Huainanzi*, grounded in a theory of sovereignty that would allow them a proprietary share in the state.

When we examine the political goals for which the early Daoist church was fighting, it was in fact for a broadening of the parameters of political participation, to allow entry for individuals whose training and competence fell outside the Confucian canon. For example, in the *Xiang'er Commentary* of the early Celestial Masters, we read,

Dao de jing: When wisdom emerged, falseness came into being.

Xiang'er Commentary: When the true Dao is hidden away, deviant writings emerge. Those mortals who commonly practice false arts proclaim them as the teachings of the Dao, but it is all fraud and may not be employed. What are these deviant writings? Of the five scriptures [that is, the Five Classics: the *Change*, *Documents*, *Odes*, *Rites*, and *Annals*], a goodly half is deviant. Beyond the five scriptures, all of the writings, biographies, and records are the creations of corpses. These are completely deviant.[131]

The *Xiang'er Commentary* argues for a broadly inclusive vision of sovereignty comparable to that of the *Huainanzi*. It does not envision a social order led by a small, select group of cognoscenti in possession of the Mandate of Heaven. Rather, its future utopia is led by a class of "transcendent nobles" into which anyone, even the most common and uneducated, can enter through a variety of techniques, many of which are closely comparable to the meditative and yogic practices advocated in the *Huainanzi*.[132]

The transition from the rarefied air of the Huainan court to the more rustic setting of the imperial periphery naturally created a shift in sensibilities and priorities among the practitioners of the arts and traditions that ultimately evolved into the Way of Supreme Peace and the Way of the Celestial Masters, the earliest Daoist church groups. Moreover, the need to conceptualize taking power from "the outside in" rather than from "the inside out" imbued the movement with populist and popularizing imperatives. The *Huainanzi* was a political manifesto pitched to elites already in control of a very wealthy and sophisticated fiscal–military state; early texts of the Daoist church such as the *Xiang'er Commentary* were written to provide the communal matrix for an army of poor farmers hoping to overthrow an established authority. However, the core practices and values around which these texts were built were parts of a single historical continuum.

Liu An never envisioned an organization like that of the Celestial Masters and would not have imagined or anticipated it. Nonetheless, if he had never launched his intellectual enterprise and the *Huainanzi* had never been written, the emergence of what we now know as the Daoist church would have been far less likely. Although never realized as the basis for the Han polity, the *Huainanzi* provided a sophisticated and elegant blueprint of how specific ideas and practices could serve as the matrix of universal empire. The accomplishment of this intellectual feat helps explain how, despite being frozen out of the halls of power, the advocates and adepts of the kinds of concepts and practices en-shrined in the *Huainanzi* kept them alive as a political ideal for so long.

"Bing lüe" Past and Present

Having looked at all the historical contexts that influenced the produc-tion of "Bing lüe" and gave shape to its unique perspective, we may well ask what it might teach those of us living today. "Bing lüe," of course, opens a window onto the past. In this sense, it and the entire *Huainanzi* text of which it is a part serve largely as a glimpse of a "road not taken" in Chinese cultural history. The *Huainanzi* obviously made an impression on the intellectual life of the Former Han, but it was never adopted as the official ideology of the dynasty, and its patron ended violently—accused of rebellion and driven to suicide by the impending arrival of imperial forces commissioned with his arrest.[133] The *Huainanzi* likely played a role in Liu An's demise. Although the text takes pains to represent itself as the words of a sage-adviser without ambitions to the throne,[134] the promulgation of a cogent, comprehensive ideology by a scion of the imperial house was an act of lèse-majesté not likely to be viewed entirely benignly by the emperor and his officials.

"Bing lüe" in particular represents a cultural cul-de-sac in certain respects. Although it presents us with what is arguably the most thoroughly "Daoist" treatment of military affairs in early Chinese letters, its ideas were not really accepted by the intellectual leaders of the Daoist church. "Bing lüe" presents a critique of the "orthodox" military perspective, arguing that the urgent need for surprise and deception underscored by texts such as the *Sunzi* created a vital military role for Daoist personal cultivation techniques, since they could imbue the commander with "spiritlike" insight. This theme was not taken up by authors writing in the tradition of the later Daoist church, however. The *Daoist Canon* (*Dao cang*) does not include a significant literature on "military methods." Even Ge Hong (283–343), the great medieval Daoist scholiast who created a syncretic summa parallel in many respects to the *Huainanzi*, did not include a separate treatment of military affairs in his *Baopuzi waipian*.[135]

This does not mean that the discussion of personal cultivation in "Bing lüe" has nothing of relevance to teach students of history today, however. The kinds of claims that "Bing lüe" (and the *Huainanzi* more generally) makes for the power and authority of apophatic personal cultivation techniques is typical of those made by many groups over the course of Chinese history, from the Yellow Turbans of the Han to the "Boxers (The Righteous and Harmonious Fists)" of the early twentieth century to the Falun Gong and many new Chinese Christian "house churches" of today. Chinese official anxiety about modern groups like the Falun Gong stems in part from the inherent political significance traditionally attributed to the kinds of personal cultivation techniques they practice, a tradition exemplified by texts such as the *Huainanzi*. This does not excuse arbitrary religious repression on the part of the Chinese or any other government, but it is a reminder that one must know something of China's cultural history if one wants to fully understand the significance of claims and practices in a Chinese social context.

Although "Bing lüe" did not initiate a tradition of Daoist military writings, other of its ideas enjoyed a more active career in imperial history. Confidence in the institution of vassalage (embodied in the maxim "sustain the perishing, revive the extinct") continued to inspire political theorists through the ages. At the founding of the Tang dynasty, arguments were asserted in favor of dividing the empire into vassal kingdoms.[136] The late Ming scholar Gu Yanwu (1613–1682) also championed the idea, arguing that a return to vassalages over "prefectures and districts" would redress the corruption and inefficiency he perceived as endemic to a centralized, bureaucratized empire.[137]

In this light, it is of interest for us in the present to situate "Bing lüe" into the history of a very long discourse about the relationship between central and local power that has engaged Chinese leaders since before the founding of the empire and continues to do so. When we examine the way in which some of the ideas forwarded in "Bing lüe" are in tension with those of other parts of the text as a whole, interesting implications emerge. Particularly, the *Huainanzi*'s general advocacy of "big government" poses a potential logical conflict with the celebration in "Bing lüe" of "sustaining the perishing, reviving the extinct." An expansion of the size and scope of the imperial government might naturally impinge on the terrain and the powers of the vassal kingdoms. Indeed, this was precisely the position advocated by many "big government" partisans in the Han, who favored the expansion of the centrally administered terrain of the empire and the reduction or outright elimination of vassal kingdoms.

What the *Huainanzi* proposes, however, is a "big government" that is expansive on all levels: the complexity and diversity of the imperial government and its personnel would be mirrored on a proportionally smaller scale at the level of the vassal kingdoms. It thus envisions an empire-wide government that is large and robust and that controls much of the economic resources and activity of society at large but is divided into regional centers that respect one another's sovereign prerogatives. In other words, the *Huainanzi* (with "Bing lüe" being a central forum in which this idea is articulated) presents us with an early Chinese ideal of federalism. While we can never know whether this specific ideal might ever have been practicable, it did seriously confront some of the intractable problems that persistently beleaguered the operation of unified rule on the scale of the Chinese empire and that continue to challenge the People's Republic of China. Those who argue that the current, super-centralized nature of the PRC is preordained by the inertia of millennia of Chinese tradition, making it impossible to find alternatives to the current status quo in areas like Taiwan, Tibet, and Xinjiang, are squarely contradicted by "Bing lüe" and the *Huainanzi* as a whole. "Bing lüe" demonstrates that the imagination of Chinese thinkers addressing questions of sovereignty and regionalism is no more limited than that of thinkers in any other human community. Cultural determinism does not doom China forever to a single principle for the relationship between central and local power.

Finally, it is of key interest to debates going on today to note that, in discussing military affairs, "Bing lüe" is most focused on *domestic* rather than foreign policy. Liu An and his clients were not interested in the potential that military assets gave the throne to project force beyond the frontier but were most concerned with the impact that the military would have on power relationships within the empire. This is a reality worth remembering in any discussion of China's military posture today. Outside observers tend to view China as a political monolith capable of drawing comprehensively on the coercive power of its society in facing the outside world, but in fact this is not now or has it ever been the case. There have always been interest groups in China, like Liu An's court, that exist in an ambivalent relationship to central power and that constrain central authority's capacity for marshaling and applying coercive force. Just as in the time of the *Huainanzi*, Chinese leaders today must calculate the effect that any military development or strategy will have on the internal stability and territorial integrity of their polity. Outside observers must take this into account when deciding how to respond to the evolving state of China's military posture.

Notes

1. The earliest sources for Liu An are his official biographies in the *Shi ji* (*Records of the Historian*) and *Han shu* (*History of the Han*). See Sima Qian 司馬遷, *Shi ji* 史記 (Beijing: Zhonghua shuju, 1959), 118:3075–94 (all citations of standard histories will be in the form chapter:pages); and Ban Gu 班固, *Han shu* 漢書 (Beijing: Zhonghua shuju, 1962), 44:2135–52. For a translation of Liu An's biography, see Burton Watson, *Records of the Grand Historian: Han Dynasty II*, rev. ed. (New York: Columbia University Press, 1993), 321–46. For a comparison of the *Han shu* and *Shi ji* biographies, see Griet Vankeerberghen, *The Huainanzi and Liu An's Claim to Moral Authority* (Albany: State University of New York Press, 2001), 153–61.

2. The kingdom of Huainan was, in Liu An's time, a vassalage extending south of the Yangtze River and covering much of present-day Anhui Province and parts of neighboring Hubei and Jiangxi provinces. For maps, see John S. Major, Sarah A. Queen, Andrew Seth Meyer, and Harold D. Roth, trans., *The Huainanzi: A Guide to the Theory and Practice of Government in Early Han China* (New York: Columbia University Press, 2010), 6.

3. For a more detailed discussion of the *Huainanzi*'s origins, see Major et al., *Huainanzi*, 1–34. The translation of "Bing lüe" in this work was originally prepared for that volume. A concise textual history of the *Huainanzi* and a bibliography of *Huainanzi* studies appear in appendix C (935–52).

4. For the early history of the Han, see Michael Loewe, "The Former Han," in *The Cambridge History of China*, vol. 1, *The Ch'in and Han Empires, 221 B.C.–A.D. 220*, ed. Denis Twitchett and Michael Loewe (Cambridge: Cambridge University Press, 1986), 103–222.

5. For a good review of the history of the Warring States, see Mark Edward Lewis, "Warring States: Political History," in *The Cambridge History of Ancient China: From the Origins of Civilization to 221 B.C.*, ed. Michael Loewe and Edward L. Shaughnessy (Cambridge: Cambridge University Press, 1999), 587–650.

6. For a study and translation of all the surviving "military classics," see Ralph D. Sawyer, *The Seven Military Classics of Ancient China* (Boulder, Colo.: Westview Press, 1993).

7. See, for example, all but the first "calendrical" essay of book seven, "The First Month of Autumn," in *Lüshi chunqiu zhuzi suoyin* 呂氏春秋逐字索引, ed. D. C. Lau 劉段爵 and Chen Fong Ching 陳方正, Institute of Chinese Studies Ancient Chinese Text Concordance Series (Hong Kong: Commercial Press, 1994), 7.2/34/5–7.5/37/16. Unless otherwise noted, all references to Masters' and military texts in this essay are to the ICS Concor-

dance Series editions. Citations are in the form chapter/page/line(s). If the ICS edition is broken into *juan* 卷 rather than *pian* 篇, the *pian* number is provided in parentheses: *juan(pian)*/page/line. The publication date of the volume is provided at the first citation. For a full translation of the *Lüshi chunqiu*, see John Knoblock and Jeffrey Riegel, *The Annals of Lü Buwei: A Complete Translation and Study* (Stanford, Calif.: Stanford University Press, 2000).

8. See, for example, "Military Methods 兵法," *Guanzi* 管子 (2001), 6.2 (17)/49/15–51/8. For a translation, see W. Allyn Rickett, *Guanzi: Political, Economic, and Philosophical Essays from Early China* (Princeton, N.J.: Princeton University Press, 1985), 1:267–78.

9. For an excellent study of the variety of military texts produced in the Warring States, see Robin D. S. Yates, "New Light on Ancient Chinese Military Texts: Notes on Their Nature and Evolution, and the Development of Military Specialization in Warring States China," *T'oung pao* 74 (1988): 211–48.

10. The title of this chapter, like almost all chapter titles in the *Huainanzi*, is evocatively ambiguous and open to multiple readings. *Lüe* means "an overview" or "a summary," but it can also mean "to plan, to strategize," and thus the title can be and often is translated as "Military Strategies." When chapter 21 of the *Huainanzi*, which summarizes the text as a whole, enumerates the chapter themes, it explains the segue from chapter 15 to chapter 16 as follows: "To know grand overviews but not know analogies and illustrations, you would lack the means to clarify affairs by elaboration" (Major et al., *Huainanzi*, 860).

This shows that the *Huainanzi* authors viewed chapter 15 as not only a treatise on military affairs but also a well-crafted literary work exemplary of an "overview" as a generic form. This was true of all the chapters between 10 and 20 of the *Huainanzi* as a whole; each is presented as exemplifying a form of written genre with which the educated emperor should be familiar. As a chapter of the *Huainanzi*, the title "Bing lüe" is thus best read as "An Overview of the Military." As a stand-alone treatise, it is best read as "Military Strategies." Throughout this essay, I refer to the title of chapter 15 by its romanized Mandarin transcription, "Bing lüe."

11. Edmund Ryden, *Philosophy of Peace in Han China: A Study of the Huainanzi Ch. 15 "On Military Strategy"* (Taipei: Taipei Ricci Institute, 1998).

12. Arthur Koestler, *Janus: A Summing Up* (New York: Random House, 1978), 2.

13. Edward L. Shaughnessy, "Western Zhou History," in *Cambridge History of Ancient China*, ed. Loewe and Shaughnessy, 292–351.

14. Li Feng, *Bureaucracy and the State in Early China: Governing the Western Zhou* (Cambridge: Cambridge University Press, 2008), 248–70. See also Constance Cook, "Wealth and the Western Zhou," *Bulletin of the School of Oriental and African Studies* 60, no. 2 (1997): 253–94.

15. Mark Edward Lewis, *Sanctioned Violence in Early China* (Albany: State University of New York Press, 1990), 36–43.

16. Li Feng, *Landscape and Power in Early China: The Crisis and Fall of the Western Zhou, 1045–771* B.C. (Cambridge: Cambridge University Press, 2006).

17. For an outline of this process of consolidation and the forces that impelled it, see Mark Edward Lewis, "Warring States: Political History," in *Cambridge History of Ancient China*, ed. Loewe and Shaughnessy, 593–616.

18. Much of the following interpretation of the development of the military texts, and especially the *Sunzi bingfa*, was first articulated by Andrew Wilson and me in Andrew Meyer and Andrew Wilson, "*Sunzi bingfa* as History and Theory," in *Strategic Logic and Political Rationality: Essays in Honor of Michael I. Handel*, ed. Bradford A. Lee and Karl F. Walling (London: Cass, 2003), 95–113.

19. Sawyer, *Seven Military Classics*, 149–51.

20. It is a matter of some dispute as to whether the *Sunzi bingfa* is the work of a single author. Some scholars have argued that it was the work of many hands, adding to a collection of aphorisms over time. This type of textual "accretion" was in fact a common phenomenon and represents the manner in which many or most Warring States texts took shape. I feel that the *Sunzi bingfa* displays a great deal of structural, logical, and thematic coherence and is thus likely the work of a single author, but it is impossible to prove either way. For convenience's sake, I refer from here on to the "author" or "composer" of the *Sunzi*, begging the reader's indulgence of this figurative device.

21. *Sunzi* 孫子 (*Bingshu sizhong zhuzi suoyin* 兵書四種逐字索引, 1992), A1/1/3. All translations are my own unless otherwise indicated.

22. The maxim is preserved in the *Zuo zhuan* 左傳, a text purporting to be a commentary to the *Spring and Autumn Annals*. The line appears in the chronicle of the thirteenth year of the reign of Duke Cheng of Lu (r. 590–573 B.C.E.): *Zuo zhuan* (1995), B8.13.2/209/19.

23. Lewis, *Sanctioned Violence*, 17–28.

24. *Mengzi* 孟子 (1995), 3.2/15/9–12, in D. C. Lau, trans., *Mencius* (London: Penguin, 1970), 76. This quote does not represent the perspective of the

Mencius but is a report of a worldview common at the time of the text's writing that is being obliquely criticized.

25. *Sunzi*, A11/12/5–6.

26. *Zuo zhuan*, Duke Xi, year 22, B5.22.8/99/1–10.

27. *Sunzi*, A6/5/7–8.

28. Edward L. Shaughnessy, "'New' Evidence of the Zhou Conquest," in *Before Confucius: Studies in the Creation of the Chinese Classics* (Albany: State University of New York Press, 1997), 35–36. The text translated here is the "Great Capture" (Shi fu) chapter of the *Yi Zhou shu*.

29. *Sunzi*, A3/2/19–20.

30. *Sunzi*, A12/13/19–22.

31. *Sunzi*, A2/1/25–29.

32. *Sunzi*, A12/13/19.

33. Much of the following interpretation was first presented by Andrew Wilson and me in Andrew Meyer and Andrew Wilson, "Inventing the General: A Reappraisal of the *Sunzi bingfa*," in *War, Virtual War, and Society: The Challenge to Communities*, ed. Andrew Wilson and Mark L. Perry (Amsterdam: Rodopi, 2008), 151–68.

34. *Sunzi*, A11/13/5–7.

35. Sawyer, *Seven Military Classics*, 183; Victor H. Mair, *The Art of War: Sun Zi's Military Methods* (New York: Columbia University Press, 2007), 124; Roger Ames, trans., *Sun-tzu: The Art of Warfare* (New York: Ballantine Books, 1993), 162.

36. For the formation of a "Masters' Literature," see Wiebke Denecke, *The Dynamics of Masters Literature: Early Chinese Thought from Confucius to Han Feizi* (Cambridge, Mass.: Harvard University Asia Center, 2011).

37. For the life and career of Confucius, see D. C. Lau, "Appendix 1: Events in the Life of Confucius," in Confucius, *The Analects*, trans. D. C. Lau (Harmondsworth: Penguin, 1979), 170–77. See also Annping Chin, *The Authentic Confucius: A Life of Thought and Politics* (New York: Scribner, 2007).

38. The novel social formation initiated by Confucius and his disciples is explored in Robert Eno, *The Confucian Creation of Heaven: Philosophy and the Defense of Ritual Mastery* (Albany: State University of New York Press, 1990), 54. See also Mark Edward Lewis, *Writing and Authority in Early China* (Albany: State University of New York Press, 1999), 55, 58.

39. It is important to note that by "Masters" in this case I refer to figures depicted in texts such as the *Analects* and *Mozi*, not actual historical individuals. In reading those texts, we are accessing the assertions of the communities

that compiled and transmitted them, not the verbatim views of the Masters they depict.

40. *Lun yu* 論語 (2006), 15.1/41/28–29. For a translation, see Confucius, *Analects*, 132.

41. *Mozi* 墨子 (2001), 5.1(17)/30/12–5.3(19)/35/28. For a translation, see Ian Johnston, *The Mozi: A Complete Translation* (New York: Columbia University Press, 2010), 166–97.

42. Their views are reported in the *Zhuangzi* 莊子 (2000), 32/99/2.

43. James J. Y. Liu, *The Chinese Knight-Errant* (Chicago: University of Chicago Press, 1967).

44. There were exceptions to the consensus I describe here. The most glaring of these was the *Guanzi* (*Master Guan*). The *Guanzi*, as noted, did contain discussions of military affairs, though these most likely postdated the *Sunzi bingfa*. The *Guanzi*, however, never depicts Master Guan taking disciples or teaching anyone other than his ruler, Duke Huan. This is because, as I have argued elsewhere, the *Guanzi* was not produced by a Master-disciple community such as that which transmitted the *Analects* but was a product of the patronage of the rulers of Qi, who were hoping to promote the organization of intellectual life around state service as opposed to "private" teaching and study. The rulers of Qi, who were aristocrats of ancient lineage, shared none of the status anxiety that motivated the compilers of the *Analects* and *Mozi*. As old aristocrats, they might have found the perspective of the military texts offensive, but they had political reasons for breaking with tradition and exploring new ideas. There is much circumstantial evidence to suggest, in fact, that the genre of military Masters' texts first flourished under Qi state patronage. See Andrew Meyer, " 'The Altars of the Soil and Grain Are Closer Than Kin': The Qi Model of Intellectual Participation and the Jixia Patronage Community," *Early China* 33 (forthcoming).

45. The epic rivalry between Wu and Yue was the subject of a whole complex of legends in ancient China. For a detailed study of this saga and its sources, see David Johnson, "Epic and History in Early China: The Matter of Wu Tzu-hsü," *Journal of Asian Studies* 40, no. 2 (1981): 255–71. See also David Johnson, "The Wu Tzu-hsü *Pien-wen* and Its Sources: Part I, Part II," *Harvard Journal of Asiatic Studies* 40, nos. 1–2 (1980): 93–156, 465–505.

46. This is argued implicitly when the text notes that the Yellow Emperor, the legendary founder of the state, had used the advantage of terrain to defeat his foes and establish the first united monarchy. See *Sunzi*, A9A/9/7–8.

47. *Sunzi*, A8/7/29.

48. *Sunzi*, A13/14/21.
49. *Lun yu*, 12.1/32/3–4, 13.3/33/27–34/3.
50. *Sunzi*, A1/1/16.
51. *Mengzi* 7.14/38/9–12, in Lau, *Mencius*, 123–24.
52. *Xunzi* 荀子 (1996), 15/68/10–12. For a full translation of the debate, see John Knoblock, *Xunzi: A Translation and Study of the Complete Works* (Stanford, Calif.: Stanford University Press, 1990), 2:211–34.
53. For the philosophy of Shen Dao, see Paul M. Thompson, *The Shen Tzu Fragments* (Oxford: Oxford University Press, 1979). For a general discussion of the use of *shi* in both military and statecraft theory, with specific attention to its use in the *Huainanzi*, see Roger Ames, *The Art of Rulership: A Study in Ancient Chinese Political Thought* (Honolulu: University of Hawai'i Press, 1983), 65–107.
54. For an in-depth study of the linguistic and philosophical implications of the concept of *shi*, see François Jullien, *The Propensity of Things: Toward a History of Efficacy in China*, trans. Janet Lloyd (New York: Zone Books, 1999).
55. This concludes the text's exposition of the three types of force and two types of heft summarized in the preceding, thus the original text for this entire discussion can be consulted in section 15.13 of the translation.
56. This is reflected in the *Shi ji* of Sima Qian, which notes knowledge of texts of "military methods" 兵法 increasingly as a practical qualification of military leaders. Among the Han founder Liu Bang's lieutenants, Zhang Liang (d. 187 B.C.E.), Ying Bu (d. 195 B.C.E), and Han Xin (d. 196 B.C.E.) were all known for their knowledge of military methods. General Wei Qing (d. 104 B.C.E.) is depicted as consulting his subordinates about military methods, and Emperor Wu is reported to have attempted to teach General Huo Qubing (d. 116 B.C.E.) the military methods of Sun Wu and Wu Qi. Liu Ci (d. 122 B.C.E.), the king of Hengshan (and Liu An's brother), is reported as seeking to recruit officers knowledgeable in military methods to aid his planned rebellion against the throne. See Sima Qian, *Shi ji*, 55:2035, 91:2606, 92:2615, 2617, 111:2927, 2939, 118:3095.
57. For the general trend to view the military as a judicial organ of state in imperial times, see Robin D. S. Yates, "Law and the Military in Early China," in *Military Culture in Imperial China*, ed. Nicola Di Cosmo (Cambridge, Mass.: Harvard University Press, 2009), 23–44.
58. For a history of the development of cosmologically oriented military texts, see Ralph Sawyer, "Martial Prognostication," in *Military Culture in Imperial China*, ed. Di Cosmo, 45–64.

59. For a detailed discussion of *ganying*, see Charles Le Blanc, *Huai-nan Tzu: Philosophical Synthesis in Early Han Thought; The Idea of Resonance (Kanying) with a Translation and Analysis of Chapter Six* (Hong Kong: Hong Kong University Press, 1985). See also John B. Henderson, *The Development and Decline of Chinese Cosmology* (New York: Columbia University Press, 1984).

60. For these early policies of the Qin, see Derk Bodde, "The State and Empire of Ch'in," in *Ch'in and Han Empires*, ed. Twitchett and Loewe, 69–72.

61. This improvisational atmosphere is exemplified by the career of Shusun Tong (d. 194 B.C.E.), a Confucian literatus and former Qin official who took up service with Liu Bang. He is said to have recommended criminals and freebooters for appointment when the Han was still engaged in military conflict, and to have cobbled together a ritual program for the Han court from ancient precedent and recent Qin practice. See *Shi ji*, 99:2720–26, translated in William H. Nienhauser, ed., *The Grand Scribe's Records*, vol. 8, *The Memoirs of Han China*, Part 1 (Bloomington: Indiana University Press, 2001), 287–93.

62. A famous example of just such a call for inclusiveness is Sima Tan's "Discourse on the Essentials of the Six Traditions," preserved in the *Shi ji* completed by his son, Sima Qian. See *Shi ji*, 130:3288–92. For the complex relationship between such rhetorical formulations and the politics of employment at the Han court, see Mark Csikszentmihalyi and Michael Nylan, "Constructing Lineages and Inventing Traditions Through Exemplary Figures in Early China," *T'oung pao* 89 (2003): 59–99.

63. For the history and background of the *Lüshi chunqiu*, see Knoblock and Riegel, *Annals of Lü Buwei*, 1–55.

64. *Lüshi chunqiu*, 12.6/62/6; Knoblock and Riegel, *Annals of Lü Buwei*, 272.

65. For the history of Lü Buwei's political career, see *Shi ji*, 85:2505–14, translated in William T. Nienhauser, ed., *The Grand Scribe's Records*, vol. 7, *The Memoirs of Pre-Han China* (Bloomington: Indiana University Press, 1995), 311–17.

66. *Huainanzi* 淮南子 (1992), 21/228/28–31; Major et al., *Huainanzi*, 867.

67. For further discussion of this root–branches concept, see Major et al., *Huainanzi*, 14–20. See also Andrew Meyer, "Root–Branches Structuralism in the *Huainanzi*," in *Text in Context: New Perspectives on the Huainanzi*, ed. Sarah Queen and Michael Puett (Leiden: Brill, forthcoming).

68. The Dao is discussed in most detail in chapter 1, "Originating in the Way," of the *Huainanzi*. See Major et al., *Huainanzi*, 41–76.

69. This root–branches cosmogony is replicated repeatedly throughout the text. See, for example, *Huainanzi*, 1/6/25–27, 2/10/14–27, 7/54/25–55/2, 14/132/10–13; Major et al., *Huainanzi*, 64–65, 84–86, 536–37.

70. *Huainanzi*, 7/55/7–10; Major et al., *Huainanzi*, 241–42.

71. *Huainanzi*, 7/59/20–23; Major et al., *Huainanzi*, 255–56.

72. *Huainanzi*, 6/52/16–53/4. This devolutionary model of human history is mirrored several times in the text. See, for example, 8/61/6–27, 8/62/6–12. Virtually the whole of chapter 13, "Boundless Discourses," is devoted to outlining this root–branches vision of history. See Major et al., *Huainanzi*, 223–25, 267–70, 271–72, 481–526.

73. This facet of the *Huainanzi*'s message is most deliberately developed in chapter 13. See Major et al., *Huainanzi*, 490–535. See also Michael Puett, *The Ambivalence of Creation: Debates Concerning Innovation and Artifice in Early China* (Stanford, Calif.: Stanford University Press, 2001), 160.

74. Ryden, *Philosophy of Peace* 9.

75. See, for example, *Guanzi*, 8.1 (19)/58/29, 16.3 (51)/118/22; *Lüshi chunqiu*, 18.1/108/24; *Xunzi*, 9/37/7; *Zhanguoce* 戰國策 (1992), 130/63/9, 249/134/2; and *Hanshi waizhuan* 韓詩外傳 (1992), 8.24/62/16.

76. Duke Huan ruled Qi during the Spring and Autumn period, after the Zhou kings had already been forced to move to their eastern capital. Since Qi was then the most militarily powerful of the vassal lords, Duke Huan's chief minister, Guan Zhong, negotiated the bestowal of the title "hegemon" on his lord by the Zhou king. The hegemon, possessing more coercive power than the king, was meant to serve as the king's proxy in disciplining the realm. He was authorized to convene meetings of the other vassal lords and to enlist their military forces in operations to put down rebellions and defend against incursions by non-Chinese peoples. The *Guanzi*, which describes Duke Huan's pursuit of a policy of "sustaining the perishing, reviving the extinct," is a Warring States text written many centuries after the lifetimes of Duke Huan and Guan Zhong.

77. *Guanzi*, 8.1 (19)/58/29; Rickett, *Guanzi*, 316.

78. For example, when he reestablished the small states of Xing, Wei, and Qii, which had been destroyed by enemy attack. See *Guanzi*, 7.1 (18)/55/12–25; Rickett, *Guanzi*, 299–305.

79. This exegetical principle is most clearly expressed in *Shi ji*, 130:3297, where it is attributed to Dong Zhongshu (179–104 B.C.E.).

80. For the early history of this development, see Herlee G. Creel, "The Beginnings of Bureaucracy in China: The Origin of the *Hsien* (*Xian*)," in *What*

Is Taoism? and Other Studies in Chinese Cultural History (Chicago: University of Chicago Press, 1970), 121–59.

81. *Shi ji*, 6:254–55.

82. Michael Loewe, *The Government of the Qin and Han Empires: 221 B.C.E.–220 C.E.* (Indianapolis: Hackett, 2006), 43–46.

83. *Shi ji*, 118:3075–81; Watson, *Records of the Grand Historian*, 321–28.

84. *Sunzi*, A11/12/11.

85. *Lüshi chunqiu*, 7.5/36/25–37/12; Knoblock and Riegel, *Annals of Lü Buwei*, 185–87.

86. Mawangdui Hanmu boshu zhengli xiaozu 馬王堆漢墓帛書整理小組, *Mawangdui Hanmu boshu* 馬王堆漢墓帛書 (Beijing: Wenwu, 1980), 45.

87. In this respect, the *Huainanzi* agrees with the *Jing fa* (*Constant Standard*), the first of five texts appended to the Laozi B manuscript discovered at Mawangdui. That text declares that "if your achievement [that is, your conquest] is complete and you do not stop, your person will be endangered and suffer calamity." Although the *Jing fa* likewise proposes that resonant forces can undo military success, as discussed earlier, it does not hold to the principle of "sustaining the perishing, reviving the extinct" (Mawangdui Hanmu boshu zhengli xiaozu, *Mawangdui Hanmu boshu*, 45).

88. For the history of Chu, see John Major and Constance Cook, eds., *Defining Chu: Image and Reality in Ancient Chin* (Honolulu: University of Hawai'i Press, 1999).

89. For the fall of Qin and the rebellion of Chen Sheng, see *Shi ji*, 48: 1949–66.

90. This is argued most explicitly in chapter 20, "The Exalted Lineage." See Major et al., *Huainanzi*, 789–840.

91. *Han shu*, 64上:2776–85. For a full translation of the memorial, see Ryden, *Philosophy of Peace*, 68–78.

92. *Han shu*, 64上:2782.

93. Ryden, *Philosophy of Peace*, 70–71.

94. The first part of this section closely parallels a passage in the *Tai gong liu tao*, but the remainder is not present in that text. See Sawyer, *Seven Military Classics*, 64–65.

95. The "feudal mound" 封 is the raised ground on which a vassal's ancestral temples are situated.

96. *Sunzi*, A8/7/29.

97. This is made explicit in chapter 8, "The Basic Warp," which states that in antiquity a campaign against an errant vassal would end with "selecting

by divination one of his sons or grandsons to replace him" (Major et al., *Huainanzi*, 286; *Huainanzi*, 8/66/21).

98. The literature on the interpretive problems surrounding the origins and nomenclature of Daoism (Taoism) is copious. Some seminal examples include Herlee G. Creel, "What Is Taoism?" in *What Is Taoism?* 1–24; Nathan Sivin, "On the Word 'Taoism' as a Source of Perplexity: With Special Reference to the Relations of Science and Religion in Traditional China," *History of Religions* 17 (1978): 303–30; Michel Strickmann, "On the Alchemy of T'ao Hung-ching," in *Facets of Taoism: Essays in Chinese Religion*, ed. Holmes Welch and Anna Seidel (New Haven, Conn.: Yale University Press, 1979), 123–92; and Kidder Smith, "Sima Tan and the Invention of Daoism, 'Legalism,' et cetera," *Journal of Asian Studies* 62, no. 1 (2003): 129–56.

99. *Shi ji*, 130:3292.

100. *Han shu*, 30:1741.

101. The *Huainanzi* claims universality for itself at several points, but most explicitly at the end of chapter 21, "An Overview of the Essentials": "We have not followed a path made by a solitary footprint, or adhered to instructions from a single perspective, or allowed ourselves to be entrapped or fettered by things so that we would not advance or shift with the age" (Major et al., *Huainanzi*, 867; *Huainanzi*, 21/228/30–31).

102. See, for example, *Lüshi chunqiu*, 3.3/14/22–24; Knoblock and Riegel, *Annals of Lü Buwei*, 105–6. This is only one example of many that could be offered. Similar arguments are made, implicitly or explicitly, in texts as diverse as the *Analects, Laozi, Mencius, Zhuangzi, Xunzi,* and *Shizi.*

103. See, for example, *Han Feizi*, 50/150/14–153/7, translated in Burton Watson, *Han Fei Tzu: Basic Writings* (New York: Columbia University Press, 1964), 118–29. Similar arguments appear in the *Mozi, Guanzi,* and other texts.

104. Major et al., *Huainanzi*, 302; *Huainanzi*, 9/69/12–17.

105. The material nature of spirit is articulated at several points in the *Huainanzi*. See, for example, *Huainanzi*, 1/9/15–16; Major et al., *Huainanzi*, 74.

106. For an account of such arguments made during a formal debate in 81 B.C.E. (the famous "Salt and Iron Debate," recorded in the *Yan tie lun*), see Michael Loewe, *Crisis and Conflict in Han China* (London: Allen & Unwin, 1974), 99–100, 109–10. Although this debate postdated the *Huainanzi*, it articulated positions that had been contended since the inception of the dynasty. For an account of contemporaries of Liu An whose views on

personal cultivation were ambivalent or hostile toward those of the *Huainanzi*, see Vankeerberghen, *Huainanzi and Liu An's Claim*, 15–27.

107. For the Confucian program of learning, see Benjamin I. Schwartz, *The World of Thought in Ancient China* (Cambridge, Mass.: Harvard University Press, 1985), 85–99; and Tu Wei-ming, *Centrality and Commonality: An Essay on Confucian Religiousness* (Albany: State University of New York Press, 1989).

108. Major et al., *Huainanzi*, 257–58; *Huainanzi*, 7/60/6–11.

109. Major et al., *Huainanzi*, 71; *Huainanzi*, 1/8/15–17.

110. For the Genuine Person in the *Huainanzi*, see Major et al., *Huainanzi*, 78, 88–89, 210, 233, 236, 280, 527, 530, 537. For the Perfected, see 78, 79–80, 233, 236, 238–39, 248–50, 252–53, 254, 259, 263, 274, 276.

111. Major et al., *Huainanzi*, 96; *Huainanzi*, 2/14/9–10.

112. Major et al., *Huainanzi*, 99; *Huainanzi*, 2/15/7.

113. For the advocacy of apophatic "inner cultivation" techniques in early (Warring States) texts, see Harold D. Roth, "Psychology and Self-Cultivation in Early Taoistic Thought," *Harvard Journal of Asiatic Studies* 51, no. 2 (1991): 599–650; and Michael LaFargue, trans., *The Tao of the Tao Te Ching: A Translation and Commentary* (Albany: State University of New York Press, 1992), 53–86. For the persistence of apophatic practice in the Daoist church, see Livia Kohn, ed., *Taoist Meditation and Longevity Techniques* (Ann Arbor: Center for Chinese Studies, University of Michigan, 1989).

114. *Sunzi*, A5/4/11–16; Sawyer, *Seven Military Classics*, 164–65.

115. See, for example, *Huainanzi*, 7/55/4, 21–24, 7/57/9, 9/72/3, 10/85/8–9; Major et al., *Huainanzi*, 241, 243, 247, 309, 360.

116. For a discussion of the broad usages of *qing* in early Chinese letters, see Michael Puett, "The Ethics of Responding Properly: The Notion of *Qing* in Early Chinese Thought," in *Love and Emotions in Traditional Chinese Literature*, ed. Halvor Eifring (Leiden: Brill, 2004), 37–68.

117. *Sunzi*, A6/5/12, 6/12; Sawyer, *Seven Military Classics*, 167, 168.

118. As the *Sunzi* declares: "One who transforms in accord with the enemy and secures victory is termed 'spiritlike'" (A6/6/12). One earns the sobriquet "spiritlike" through victory. In the *Huainanzi*, the causal relationship is reversed: one secures victory by becoming a spiritlike individual.

119. Wang Liqi 王利器, *Yan tie lun jiaozhu* 鹽鐵論校注 (Beijing: Zhonghua shuju, 1992), 405.

120. Wang Liqi, *Yan tie lun jiaozhu*, 406.

121. Wang Liqi, *Yan tie lun jiaozhu*, 410.

122. Wang Liqi, *Yan tie lun jiaozhu*, 410–11.

123. For the early history of the Mandate, see Herrlee G. Creel, *The Origins of Statecraft in China* (Chicago: University of Chicago Press, 1970), 81–100.

124. Su Yu 蘇輿, *Chunqiu fanlu yizheng* 春秋繁露義證 (Beijing: Zhonghua shuju, 1992), 319.

125. *Huainanzi*, 9/72/4–10; Major et al., *Huainanzi*, 310.

126. *Huainanzi*, 9/74/18–20; Major et al., *Huainanzi*, 317.

127. *Huainanzi*, 13/120/3–5; Major et al., *Huainanzi*, 490.

128. *Huainanzi*, 13/124/7–8; Major et al., *Huainanzi*, 502.

129. Ban Gu, *Han shu*, 75:3192.

130. For *fang shi*, see Kenneth J. DeWoskin, *Doctors, Diviners, and Magicians of Ancient China: Biographies of Fang-shih* (New York: Columbia University Press, 1983).

131. Stephen Bokenkamp, trans., *Early Daoist Scriptures* (Berkeley: University of California Press, 1996), 104–5.

132. Bokenkamp, *Early Daoist Scriptures*, 41–42, 57–58, 97, 104, 110–13, 135.

133. *Shi ji*, 118:3094; Watson, *Records of the Grand Historian*, 346.

134. This is argued all but explicitly in chapter 21, "An Overview of the Essentials," which lists among the forebears of the *Huainanzi* series of nonrulers who had served as the ideological authorities of successive governments the Grand Duke, the Duke of Zhou, Guan Zhong, Confucius, and others. See Major et al., *Huainanzi*, 862–67; *Huainanzi*, 21/227/20–228/31.

135. Jay Sailey, *The Master Who Embraces Simplicity: A Study of the Philosopher Ko Hung, A.D. 283–343* (San Francisco: Chinese Materials Center, 1978). A possible exception to this trend is the commentaries of the Tang scholar Li Quan 李筌 (fl. mid-eighth century C.E.) to the *Laozi* and *Huangdi yinfu jing*, which express ideas similar to those of "Bing lüe." See Christopher C. Rand, "Li Ch'üan and Chinese Military Thought," *Harvard Journal of Asiatic Studies* 39, no. 1 (1979): 107–37. The long interval between these texts makes the relationship between them tentative, however.

136. David McMullen, *State and Scholars in T'ang China* (Cambridge: Cambridge University Press, 1988), 170, 186, 196–97.

137. Gu Yanwu 顧炎武, *Gu Tinglin shiwen ji* 顧亭林詩文集 (Beijing: Zhonghua shuju, 1983), 12–17.

An
OVERVIEW
of the
MILITARY

15.1

In antiquity, those who used the military did not value expanding territory or covet the possession of gold and jade. They sought to sustain those who [were] perishing, revive those [lineages] that had been cut off,[1] pacify the chaos of the world, and eliminate harm to the myriad people.

All beasts that have blood and *qi*,[2]
are equipped with teeth and horns.
They have claws in front and paws behind.
Those with horns gore;
those with teeth bite;
those with poison sting;
those with hooves kick.
When they are happy, they play with one another;
when they are angry they injure one another;
this is their Heaven[-born] nature.

1. The phrase "sustain those that are perishing and revive those that had become extinct" (*cun wang ji jue* 存亡繼絶) is used in the *Chunqiu Guliang zhuan* 春秋股梁傳, Duke Xi, year 17, to describe the merit of Duke Huan of Qi.
2. *Qi* is both matter and energy, the basic stuff out of which the entire universe is composed. All things, including the bodies of living creatures, are composed of and animated by *qi* in various states of rarefaction. See the introduction to this volume.

Humans have instincts for clothing and food, yet [material] things are lacking. Thus they settle together in various locations. If the division is not equal, if demands are not fulfilled, they fight. When they fight, the strong threaten the weak and the brave attack the cowardly. People do not have strong muscles and bones or sharp claws and teeth, thus

> they cut leather to make armor;
> they forge iron to make blades.

Greedy and cruel people brutalize and rob the world. The myriad people are shaken; they cannot rest in tranquillity with what they possess. The sage rises up vehemently, punishing the strong and the violent [and] pacifying the chaotic age. He suppresses danger and eliminates disorder.

> He makes the sullied pure;
> he makes the imperiled calm.

Thus people are not cut off in mid[life].
The origins of the military are distant!

> The Yellow Emperor once warred with Yan Di;[3]
> Zhuan Xu once fought with Gong Gong.[4]
> The Yellow Emperor warred in the wilds of Zhuolu;[5]
> Yao warred on the banks of the River Dan;[6]

---

3. The primeval conflict between the Yellow Emperor and Yan Di is mentioned in *Lüshi chuhqiu* 7.2. The Yellow Emperor 黃帝 was a legendary ruler of high antiquity, often credited with being the inventor of the state. Yan Di 炎帝, the "Flame Emperor," is a semidivine figure who figures variously in different myths. In some stories, he is credited with having invented the use of fire for humankind; in others, he is depicted as a rebel against the legitimate authority of the Yellow Emperor, who is sometimes identified as his half brother.

4. Gong Gong 共工 is a mythical figure of high antiquity, sometimes described as the "minister of works" to the ancient thearchs but also depicted as a rebel and fomenter of disorder. Zhuan Xu 顓頊 is a divine thearch and god of the north, from whom many aristocratic lineages of the Bronze Age claimed descent.

5. This refers to the ancient battle between the Yellow Emperor and Chi You. See *Zhuangzi* 29. Chi You 蚩尤 was a legendary rebel sometimes credited with having initiated war in human history.

6. *Lüshi chunqiu* 20.4 records a campaign by Yao against the Southern Man on the River Dan. Yao 堯 was a legendary sage king of high antiquity, famous for having abdicated the throne to his most able minister, Shun 舜.

Shun attacked the Youmiao;[7]
Qi attacked the Youhu.[8]

Since the time of the Five Thearchs, [no one] has been able to ban [the military], much less in a declining age! [15/142/21–29]

15.2

The military sees to it that the violent are curtailed and the disorderly [are] punished.

> Yandi created a conflagration, thus the Yellow Emperor captured him;
>
> Gong Gong created a flood, thus Zhuan Xu executed him.

If one teaches them the Way, guides them with Potency but they do not listen, then one displays martial might to them. If one displays martial might to them but they do not obey, one controls them with weapons and armor. Thus the sage's use of the military is like combing hair or weeding seedlings; those he eliminates are few, [and] those he benefits are many.

> There is no harm greater than killing innocent people to support an unrighteous king;
>
> there is no calamity more profound than to exhaust the wealth of the world to satisfy one person's desires.
>
> If [King] Jie of Xia and [King] Djou of Yin had met with calamity as soon as they harmed the people, they would not have reached [the point of] creating the "roasting beam."[9]
>
> If [Duke] Li of Jin and [King] Kang of Song had [met with] the death of their persons and the destruction of their states as soon

---

7. Shun's campaign against the Youmiao 有苗 (Miao) is recorded in the "Shun dian" chapter of the *Documents*.
8. Qi's campaign against the Youhu 有扈 is recorded in the "Gan shi" chapter of the *Documents*. Qi 啟, mythical son of Yu the Great, succeeded his father as the king of the Xia dynasty.
9. The "roasting beam" was a cruel punishment famously associated with King Djou 紂, the wicked last ruler of the Shang 商 dynasty (ca. 1766–1045 B.C.E.). King Jie 桀 was the wicked last ruler of the legendary Xia dynasty, which preceded the Shang.

as they committed one act of unrighteousness, they would not have reached the point of invading and conquering or unleashing tyranny.[10]

These four rulers all committed small transgressions and were not punished, thus they arrived at unsettling the world, harming the common people [and] extending the calamity of the realm by giving free rein to a single man's deviance. This is what the standard of Heaven will not accept. A ruler is established in order to curtail the violent and punish the disorderly. Now if one commands the strength of the myriad people yet conversely commits cruelty and robbery, this is like a tiger sprouting wings. How can it not be eliminated? [15/143/1–8]

One who raises fish in a pond must fend off otters;
one who raises birds and animals must likewise fend off wolves.

How much more so the one who governs people!

Thus the military of a hegemon or king

is given forethought according to standards,
is planned for according to strategy,
is applied according to Rightness.

It is not used to destroy those that survive
[but] to sustain [those that] are perishing.

When he hears that the ruler of an enemy state is being cruel to his people, he raises the military and descends on [the enemy's] borders.

He blames the enemy for his lack of Rightness;
he criticizes him for his excessive actions.

When the military reaches the suburbs [of the enemy capital], he commands the army, saying:

"Do not cut down trees;
do not disturb graves;
do not scorch the five grains;
do not burn property;
do not take the people as slaves;

---

10. Duke Li of Jin 晉厲公 reigned the Zhou vassalage of Jin from 580 to 573 B.C.E. King Kang of Song 宋康王 (r. 328–286 B.C.E.) was the last ruler of the state of Song. Both men were comparable to the tyrants Jie and Djou for their avarice and profligacy.

do not steal the six domestic animals."

Then he issues a pronouncement and effects an edict, saying, "The ruler of X kingdom has scorned Heaven and insulted the ghosts.

He has imprisoned the innocent;
he has wrongfully executed the blameless.
This is what is punished by Heaven,
what is hated by the people.

The coming of the military is to cast aside the unrighteous and to restore the virtuous. Anyone who opposes the Way of Heaven and leads those who rob the people will be killed and his clan exterminated.

Anyone who leads his family to obey will be given an income for his household;
anyone who leads his village to obey will be rewarded with [control of] his village;
anyone who leads his town to obey will be given his town as a fief.
Anyone who leads his district to obey will be made marquis of his district."

His conquest of the kingdom does not touch the people; he [only] discards their ruler and changes their government.

He reveres their excellent scholars and gives prominence to the worthy and the good;
he uplifts their orphans and widows and shows compassion to their poor and desperate.
He releases those [unjustly] imprisoned;
he rewards those who have merit.

The common people open their doors and await him; they cook rice and supply him; only fearing that he will not come.[11]

This was how Tang and Wu became kings[12]

---

11. This section roughly parallels text found in *Lüshi chunqiu* 7.5/36/25–37/12. See John Knoblock and Jeffrey Riegel, *The Annals of Lü Buwei: A Complete Translation and Study* (Stanford, Calif.: Stanford University Press, 2000), 185–87.

12. Tang, or Cheng Tang 成湯, was the legendary founding sage-king of the Shang dynasty. Wu 武 (r. 1045–1043 B.C.E.) was the second king of the Zhou 周 dynasty (1045–256 B.C.E.). It was he who conquered the Shang after his father, King Wen 文 (r. 1056–1050 B.C.E.), died in the midst of their righteous rebellion.

and how [Duke] Huan of Qi and [Duke] Wen of Jin became hegemons.[13]

Thus when the ruler is without the Way, the people yearn for the military [just] as they hope for rain during a drought or plead for water when they are thirsty. Who among them will lift a weapon to meet the military? Thus to conclude without battle is the ultimate of the righteous military. [15/143/10–21]

15.3

In regard to the military of later ages, although rulers may be without the Way, none do not dig moats, build battlements, and defend [them]. Those who attack do not do so to curtail violence or eliminate harm; they want to invade the land and expand their territory. For this reason, the bodies pile up and the blood flows; they face one another all day, yet the achievement of a hegemon does not appear in the age. It is because they act selfishly.

One who wars for territory cannot become a king;

one who wars for himself cannot establish his merit.

One who takes up a task on behalf of others will be aided by the multitude;

one who takes up a task on his own behalf will be discarded by the multitude.

One who is aided by the multitude must [become] strong even if he is weak;

one who is discarded by the multitude must perish even if he is great. [15/143/23–26]

The military is

weak if it loses the Way;

strong if it obtains the Way.

---

13. Duke Huan of Qi 齊桓公 (r. 685–643 B.C.E.) and Duke Wen of Jin 晉文公 (r. 636–628 B.C.E.) were exemplary rulers of the Spring and Autumn period 春秋 (771–481 B.C.E.). They were the first and second figures, respectively, to occupy the post of *ba* 霸, or "hegemon."

The commander is
>inept if he loses the Way;
>skillful if he obtains the Way.

The state will
>survive if it obtains the Way;
>perish if it loses the Way.

What is called the Way
>embodies the circle and is modeled on the square,
>shoulders the yin and embraces the yang,
>is soft on the left and hard on the right,
>treads in the obscure and carries illumination.

It alters and transforms without constancy; it obtains the source of the One and thereby responds limitlessly. This is called spirit illumination.

>The circle is Heaven;
>the square is earth.

>Heaven is circular and without terminus, thus one cannot view its form;
>the earth is square and without boundaries, thus one cannot see its gateway.

>Heaven transforms and nurtures yet is without form;
>Earth generates and rears and yet is without measure.

Vague, hazy, who knows their capacity?

All things have that which defeats them;[14] only the Way is invincible.[15] It is invincible because it has no constant shape or force. It cycles ceaselessly, like the motion of the sun and moon.

>Just as summer and autumn alternate,
>just as the sun and the moon have day and night,
>it reaches an end and begins again;
>it illuminates and becomes dark again.

---

14. Following Wang Shumin 王叔岷's proposed emendation. See D. C. Lau 劉段爵 and Chen Fong Ching 陳方正, eds., *Huainanzi zhuzi suoyin* 淮南子逐字索引, Institute of Chinese Studies Ancient Chinese Text Concordance Series (Hong Kong: Commercial Press, 1992), 144n.3.

15. Following Wang Shumin's proposed emendation. See Lau and Chen, *Huainanzi zhuzi suoyin*, 144n.4.

None can attain its pattern. [15/144/1–7]
>It controls form yet is formless;
>thus its merit can be complete.
>It objectifies things yet is no object;
>thus it triumphs and does not submit. [15/144/9]

15.4

Form/punishment[16] is the ultimate of the military. Arriving at being without form/punishment may be called the ultimate of the ultimate. For this reason, the great military does no injury; it communicates with the ghosts and spirits. It does not brandish the five weapons, [yet] none in the world dares oppose it. It sets up its drums [but] does not open its arsenal, and none of the Lords of the Land do not freeze in terror. Thus
>one who wars from the temple becomes emperor;[17]
>one who [effects] spirit transformation becomes king.
What is called "warring from the temple" is modeling [oneself] on the Way of Heaven.
Spirit transformation is modeling [oneself] on the four seasons.
>He cultivates governance within his borders and those afar long
>for his Potency;
>he achieves victory without battle, and the Lords of the Land submit to his might.
It is because internally his government is ordered. [15/144/9–12]
In antiquity those who obtained the Way
>in stillness modeled [themselves] on Heaven and Earth,

---

16. This is a deliberate pun. The character translated (*xing* 刑) means both "form" (形) and "punishment," and both meanings are being invoked here. The latter sense is that punishing wrongdoing is the ultimate end of the military, but the ultimate fulfillment of this end is achieved when punishments are no longer necessary. The former sense is that "form" (the formation of the army in battle, the form of plans and operations) is the ultimate arbiter of success for the military, but achieving a state of "formlessness" (or accessing the power of the Formless) is the ultimate embodiment of martial skill.

17. "Warring from the temple" 廟戰 alludes to the first chapter of the *Sunzi bingfa*, which discusses the calculations made in the ancestral temple before battle has been joined. The basic notion here is that victory is achieved in the careful preparation before the battle, not in heroics on the field of battle itself.

in motion complied with the sun and moon.

In delight and anger they corresponded to the four seasons;
in calling and answering they were comparable to the thunder and lightning.

Their voice and breath did not oppose the eight winds;
their contracting and extending did not exceed the five standards.[18]

Below to those [creatures] that have armor and scales;
above to those that have fur and feathers;

all were ordered from first to last. Among the myriad creatures and the hundred clans, from beginning to end, none was without its proper place. For this reason,

[the Way] enters what is small without being pressed,
lodges in what is vast without being exposed.

It seeps into metal and stone;
it washes over grasses and trees.

[From] something that expands to fill the limits of the six coordinates to the end of a single hair, nothing does not cleave to it. The penetration of the Way suffuses what is [most] subtle. There is nowhere it does not reside; this is why it triumphs over the powerful and the many. [15/144/14–18]

15.5

In archery, if the calibration of the sights is not correct, the target will not be hit.

With the thoroughbred, if [even] one tally goes unused, one thousand *li* will not be reached.[19]

---

18. Compare the "five positions" (*wu wei* 五位) in *Huainanzi* 5.13. See John S. Major, Sarah A. Queen, Andrew Seth Meyer, and Harold D. Roth, trans., *The Huainanzi: A Guide to the Theory and Practice of Government in Early Han China* (New York: Columbia University Press, 2010), 200–202.

19. "Thoroughbred" (*ji* 驥) is literally a horse capable of traversing a thousand *li* in a single day. One *li* is an early Chinese unit of distance, equivalent to approximately one-third of a mile (0.4 kilometer). The point here is that despite its remarkable talents, the thoroughbred cannot complete the journey unless its rider is equipped beforehand with all the official tallies that will afford passage through government gate stations along the way.

Being defeated in battle does not happen on the day the drums give the order [to advance]; one's daily conduct has been without discipline for a long time. Thus in the military that has obtained the Way,

the chocks are not removed from the chariot [wheels];
the mounts are not saddled;
the drums raise no dust;
the banners are not unfurled;
the armor is not removed from its casings;[20]
the blades do not taste blood;
the court does not shift its location;
the merchants do not leave the market;
the farmers do not leave the fields.

When [the ruler] issues a righteous summons and charges them,

large kingdoms pay court;
small cities submit.

He follows people's desires and marshals the people's strength by eliminating cruelty and dispelling thievery.

Thus,

those who value the same [thing] will die for one another;
those who share the same feelings complete one another;
those who have the same desires will find one another;
those who hate the same thing will assist one another.
If one moves in compliance with the Way, the world will [respond as] an echo.
If one plans in compliance with the people, the world will be one's weapon.

When hunters are pursuing game, the chariots race and the men run, each exhausting his strength. There is no threat of punishment, yet they scold one another for stumbling and urge one another on because they [all] will share in the benefit.

When those in the same boat are crossing a river and meet suddenly with wind and waves, the sons of the hundred clans all quickly grab

---

20. Following Zhang Shuangdi 張雙棣, *Huainanzi jiaoshi* 淮南子校释 (Beijing: Beijing University Press, 1997), 2:1558n.22.

the oars and row the vessel,[21] as if they were the right and left hands [of
a single person]. They do not contend with one another because they
share the same distress.

Thus the enlightened king's use of the military is to eliminate injury
to the world, and he shares its benefits with the people. The people
work as sons do for their fathers, as younger brothers for their elder
brothers. The impact of [the king's] might is like a mountain collaps-
ing or a dike bursting, what enemy would dare to oppose him? Thus,
he who excels at using the military uses [the people] for their own
sakes.

> If you use [people] for their own sakes, then none in the world
> may not be used.
> If you use [people] for your own sake, what you achieve will be
> scanty. [15/144/20–29]

15.6

The military has three foundations:
> In ordering the kingdom, regulate within the borders.
> In effecting Humaneness and Rightness, spread Moral Potency
> and Benevolence.
> In establishing correct laws, block deviant paths.[22]

[When]
> the collected ministers are intimately close;
> the common people are harmonious;
> superiors and inferiors are of a single mind;
> ruler and minister unite their efforts.
> The Lords of the Land submit to your might and the four direc-
> tions cherish your Moral Potency;

21. Following the reading of Yang Shuda 楊樹達. See Zhang, *Huainanzi jiaoshi*,
    2:1559n.26.
22. In accordance with William Boltz's (private communication) identification of the
    rhyme scheme, preserving *sui* 隧, instead of Lau and Chen's (*Huainanzi zhuzi suoyin*,
    15/145/1) suggested emendation to *dao* 道.

you cultivate governance in the temple hall and extend control
    beyond one thousand *li*;
you fold your hands, issue commands, and the world responds as
    an echo.
This is the highest use of the military.
[When]
    the territory is broad and the people numerous;
    the ruler is worthy and the commanders loyal;
    the kingdom is rich and the military strong;
    covenants and prohibitions are trustworthy;
    pronouncements and orders are clear.
    The two armies oppose each other;
    the bells and drums face each other;
yet the enemy flees before the soldiers meet or blades clash. This is the
middling use of the military.
[When]
    you understand what suits the terrain,
    practice the beneficial [use of] narrow and obstructed [posi-
        tions],
    discern the alterations of the extraordinary and the usual,[23]
    investigate the rules for marching and formation, dispersion and
        concentration;
    bind the drumsticks [to your forearms] and roll the drums.
    White blades meet;
    flying arrows are exchanged;
    you wade through blood and tread through guts;
    you cart the dead away and support the wounded;
    the blood flows for a thousand *li*;
    exposed corpses fill the field;

---

23. *Qi* 奇 and *zheng* 正 are used here in a special technical sense established by military
texts like the *Sunzi bingfa*. "Extraordinary" and "usual" refer to the commander's se-
lective and timely use of surprise tactics that break with conventional military doctrine. Both terms are discussed at length in Victor Mair, *The Art of War: Sun Zi's Military Methods* (New York: Columbia University Press, 2007), and *Soldierly Methods:
Vade Mecum for an Iconoclastic Translation of Sun Zi bingfa*, Sino-Platonic Papers,
no. 178 (Philadelphia: Department of Asian Languages and Civilizations, University
of Pennsylvania, 2008).

thus victory is decided. This is the lowest use of the military.
Now everyone in the world
>knows to work at studying its branches,
>and none knows to resolve to cultivate its root.

This is to discard the root and plant the limbs. [15/145/1–8]

Those things that assist the military in victory are many; those that ensure victory are few.

>If armor is sturdy and weapons sharp,
>chariots are solid and horses excellent,
>rations and equipment sufficient,
>officers and men numerous,

these are the great foundations of the army, yet victory is not [found] here. If one is clear about

>the movements of the stars, planets, sun, and moon;
>the rules of recision and accretion[24] and the occult arts;[25]
>the advantages of the rear, front, left, and right;

these are aids to warfare, yet completeness is not [found] here.

That by which the excellent commander is ensured victory is his constant possession of a knowledge without origin, a Way that is not a Way. It is difficult to share with the multitude. [15/145/10–13]

15.7

>Meticulously recruiting [personnel],
>timeliness in movement and rest,

---

24. Here *xingde* 刑德 is not used in the conventional sense of "punishment and benefi-cence" but refers to the recision and accretion of yin and yang as seen in various cosmic cycles, especially the cycle of lengthening and shortening days throughout the solar year. See *Huainanzi* 3.16 and 3.17. Accretion and recision are mentioned in the context of military astrology in *Huainanzi* 3.33 and 3.39, where the directional movements of counter-Jupiter (*taiyin*) are linked to victory or defeat. See John S. Ma-jor, *Heaven and Earth in Early Han Thought: Chapters Three, Four, and Five of the Huainanzi* (Albany: State University of New York Press, 1993), 122–26, 132–33.

25. The phrase *qi gai zhi shu* 奇賌之數 is somewhat obscure. I follow the commentaries compiled in Zhang, *Huainanzi jiaoshi*, 2:1564n.12, in rendering it as "occult arts." Xu Shen 許慎 glosses it as "the strange and secret essentials of yin and yang, extraordi-nary arts."

distinguishing officers and enlisted men,
maintaining weapons and armor,
ordering marching squadrons,
organizing platoons and companies,
clarifying drum and banner [signals],
these are the office of the adjutant.[26]
Distinguishing army camps,
scouring the terrain thoroughly,
choosing the location of the army,
these are the office of the master of horse.
Knowing [which terrain] is obstructed or passable to the front or
the rear;
on encountering the enemy knowing what is difficult or easy;
issuing reprimands so that there is no negligence or idleness;
this is the office of the commandant.
[Ensuring that] movement along the route is swift,
that transport of the baggage is orderly,
that the size [of the camp] is standard,
that the positioning of the army is concentrated,
that the wells and stoves are dug [properly],
these are the office of the master of works.
Collecting and storing [materials] in the rear,
leaving nothing behind when camp is moved,
that there are no poorly packed carts,
that there is no missing baggage,
these are the office of the quartermaster.
These five officers are to the commander as the arms, legs, hands,
and feet are to the body. He must choose men, assess their talents,
[and] make sure that [each] officer can shoulder his responsibilities
[and each] man is capable of his task.
He instructs them with regulations;
he applies them with orders;
using them the way that

---

26. This reading rejects Lau and Chen's (*Huainanzi zhuzi suoyin*, 15/145/13) proposed
interpolation of *da* to read the title as *dawei* (大尉 = 太]尉), or "defender-in-chief"
(a court office). All five offices listed here are army ranks, not court offices.

tigers and leopards use their claws and teeth;
flying birds use their wings.
None is not employed. However, they all are implements that assist
victory; they are not that by which victory is ensured. [15/145/13–19]

15.8

The victory or defeat of the military has its basis in governance.

> If governance overcomes the people, subordinates will follow
> their superiors, and the military will be strong.
> If the people overcome [their] government, subordinates will
> rebel against their superiors, and the military will be weak.

Thus,

> if Moral Potency and Rightness are sufficient to encompass the
> people of the world,
> if tasks and works are sufficient to meet the urgency of the world,
> if selection and promotion are sufficient to win the minds of the
> worthies and scholars,
> if plans and designs suffice to comprehend the heft of strength
> and weakness,

this is the root of certain victory. [15/145/19–21]

> Vast territory and numerous people do not suffice to make one
> strong;
> sturdy armor and sharp weapons do not suffice to make one vic-
> torious;
> high walls and deep moats do not suffice to make one secure;
> strict orders and complex punishments do not suffice to make
> one mighty.
> One who practices the governance of survival, though [his king-
> dom] is small, will certainly survive.
> One who practices the governance of extinction, though [his
> kingdom] is large, will certainly perish.

In antiquity, the territory of the Kingdom of Chu [27]

---

27. Ancient Chu spanned western Hubei and southwestern Henan Province. The geo-
graphical frontiers listed in this passage fall within or border on that general region.

on the south was ringed by the Yuan and Xiang [rivers],
on the north was circled by the Ying and Si [rivers],
on the west was contained by [the states of] Ba and Shu,
on the east, was wrapped by [the states of] Tan and Pi.
[It had] the Ying and Ru [rivers] as ditches;
the Yangzi and Han [rivers] as moats.
Fenced in by the Deng Forest,
screened by a defensive wall.
The mountains [were] so high they scraped the clouds;
the valleys so deep there were no shadows.
The terrain advantageous, the conditions favorable;
the soldiers and people courageous and daring.
They had shark's leather and rhinoceros [hide] to make armor
and helmets;
they had long halberds and short spears together to make up the
vanguard.
They had repeating crossbows to bring up the rear,
massed chariots to guard the flanks.
At the quick they were like bolts and arrows,[28]
concentrated they were like thunder and lightning,
dispersed they were like the wind and rain.
However,
their soldiers fell at Chuisha;[29]
their multitudes were broken at Boju.[30]
The might of Chu spanned the earth and encompassed the masses;
their portion was half the world. Yet King Huai feared Lord Mengchang
to the north,[31] [so] he abandoned the defense of his ancestral altars and

---

28. There seems to be one part of the parallelism missing here. "Concentrated" and "dispersed" (in the following two lines) are in parallel, so immediately after this line there
should be a phrase parallel with "at the quick."

29. Chu was defeated by the combined armies of Qin, Han, Wei, and Qi at Chuisha in
301 B.C.E. The event is recorded in *Xunzi* 15 and *Zhanguoce* 179.

30. Chu was defeated by the combined armies of Cai and Wu at Boju in 506 B.C.E. See
Zuozhuan, Duke Ding, year 4.

31. King Huai of Chu 楚懷王 reigned from 328 to 299 B.C.E. Lord Mengchang 孟嘗君
(also known as Tian Wen 田文 [ca. 330–ca. 280 B.C.E.]) was a powerful scion of the
royal house of Qi. He was renowned as a great patron and statesman; his biography is
recounted in detail in *Shiji* 75.

became a hostage of mighty Qin. His soldiers defeated and his territory pared away, he died without returning home.

The Second Emperor [of Qin][32] had the force of the Son of Heaven and the wealth of the world.

Nowhere that human footprints reached
or that was traversed by boat and oar

was not his prefecture or district.

Yet,

he was ensnared in the desires of the ears and eyes;
he practiced every possible variety of license and wickedness.

He paid no heed to the people's hunger, cold, poverty, and distress. He raised a chariot force of ten thousand chariots and built the A-fang palace; he

dispatched conscripted villagers for garrison duty
and collected taxes of more than half [income].

Those among the common people who were conscripted or executed, who died gripping the crossbar of a wagon or at the head of the road, numbered countless myriads every day.

The world

was feverish as if scorching hot,
bent as if bitterly belabored.
Superior and inferior were not at peace with each other;
officials and commoners were not in harmony.

Chen Sheng,[33] a conscript soldier, arose in Daze. He bared his right arm and raised it, proclaiming himself "Great Chu," and the empire responded like an echo. At that time, he did not have

strong armor or sharp weapons,
powerful bows or hard spears.
They cut date trees to make spears;
they ground awls and chisels to make swords.

---

32. The Second Emperor 二世皇帝, or Hu Hai 胡亥, was the son and heir of the First Emperor of Qin. He reigned from 210 B.C.E. until his death by suicide in 207 B.C.E.

33. Chen Sheng 陳勝 (d. 208 B.C.E.) was a minor Qin official who initiated the uprising that brought down the Qin dynasty. He is commemorated with his own "Hereditary House" in *Shiji* 48.

They sharpened bamboo
and shouldered hoes

to meet keen halberds and strong crossbows, [yet] no city they attacked or land they invaded did not surrender to them. They roiled and shook, overran and rolled up an area of several thousand square *li* throughout the world. [Chen Sheng's] force and station were supremely lowly, and his weapons and equipment were of no advantage, yet one man sang out and the empire harmonized with him. This was because resentment had accumulated among the people. [15/145/23–15/146/12]

When King Wu attacked Djou, he faced east and welcomed the year.[34]

When he reached the Si River, there was a flood;
when he reached Gongtou, [a mountain] collapsed.[35]

A comet appeared and presented its tail to the men of Yin [i.e., Shang]. During the battle;

ten suns rioted above;
wind and rain struck below.[36]

Yet,

in front there were no rewards for braving danger;
at the rear there were no punishments for flight.

Clean blades were never fully drawn and the empire submitted. For this reason,

he who is good at defending cannot be overcome,
and he who is good at battle cannot be attacked.

He understands the Way of restricting entries and opening blockages. He takes advantage of the force of the moment, accords with the desires of the people, and seizes the world. [15/146/14–17]

----

34. This ritual was performed to mark the beginning of spring. It is presumably noted here to demonstrate that the following events occurred out of season. What follows are a sequence of bad auguries for the endeavor of King Wu, despite which he prevails because of his superior Moral Potency.

35. Following Wang Shumin's emendation. See Lau and Chen, *Huainanzi zhuzi suoyin*, 146n.13.

36. Following Wang Shumin's emendation. See Lau and Chen, *Huainanzi zhuzi suoyin*, 146n.14.

15.9

Thus,

> one who is good at governing accumulates Moral Potency;
> one who is good at using the military stores anger.
> When Moral Potency accumulates, the people may be employed;
> when anger is stored, one's awesomeness may be established.

Thus,

> when one's culture has been applied shallowly, what is brought to
> submission by heft will be meager.
> If one's Potency functions broadly, what is controlled by one's
> awesomeness will be expansive.
> When what is controlled by one's awesomeness is broad, I am
> strong and the enemy is weak.

Therefore, one who is good at using the military first weakens the enemy and only after does battle. In this way the expense is not even half, and the effect is naturally doubled.

> The territory of Tang was seventy *li* square, and he became king.
> This was because he cultivated his Moral Potency.
> Earl Zhi had one thousand *li* of land and perished. This was
> because he was exclusively martial.[37]

Thus,

> a thousand-chariot state that practices culture and Potency will
> become king;
> a ten-thousand chariot state that is fond of using the military will
> perish.

Thus,

> a complete soldier is first victorious and only then seeks battle;
> a defeated soldier gives battle first and only then seeks victory.
> If Potency is equal, the many will defeat the few.

---

37. Earl Zhi 知伯 (also known as Earl Yao 瑤 of Zhi [d. 453 B.C.E.]) was a colorful figure whose tale is recounted in many texts as an example of overreaching ambition. As leader of the Zhi clan, he seemed poised to bring all the vassal clans of Jin under his sway, until his overbearing belligerence drove the Han, Wei, and Zhao clans to unite to destroy him.

If strength is matched, the intelligent will defeat the stupid.

If intelligence is the same, then the one with numbers will capture the one without. In all use of the military, one must first fight from the temple.

> Whose ruler is more worthy?
> Whose commander is more able?
> Whose people are more obedient?
> Whose state is better ordered?
> Who has prepared more stores?
> Whose troops are better trained?
> Whose armor and weapons are better?
> Whose equipment is more efficient?

In this way, one moves counters in the upper hall of the temple and decides victory more than a thousand miles away. [15/146/19–26]

15.10

> What has form and outline will be seen and praised by the world;
> what has chapter and verse will be transmitted and studied by the
>   ages.

These all are [examples] of forms overcoming one another. The one who is skilled at form does not use them as a model. What ennobles the Way is its formlessness. Having no form, it thus

> cannot be controlled or coerced;
> it cannot be measured or ruled;
> it cannot be tricked or deceived;
> it cannot be schemed against or planned for.
> People will make plans for one whose wisdom is apparent;
> they will attack one whose form is apparent;
> they will ambush one whose numbers are apparent;
> they will defend against one whose weapons are apparent.

Those who

> move and initiate, circulate and turn,
> straighten and bend, contract and extend.

may be tricked and deceived; none is skilled. The movement of the skilled
> is as apparent as that of a spirit and yet proceeds like that of a ghost,
> is as brilliant as the stars and yet operates in obscurity.

Advancing and retreating, contracting and extending, none sees its form or outline.
> It alights like the halcyon and rises like the unicorn,
> flies like the phoenix and leaps like the dragon.
> It emerges like a gale;
> it speeds like lightning.
> it beats death with life;
> it overcomes decline with virility;
> it defeats torpor with speed;
> it controls hunger with fullness.
> Like water eradicating fire,
> like heat melting snow.
> Where can one go where it does not follow?
> Where can one move where it does not reach?
> Within, empty and spiritlike;
> without, barren of will;
> it moves in the formless;
> it emerges where it is not expected;
> it leaves tumultuously;
> it returns unexpectedly.

None knows its destination.
> Sudden as thunder and lightning,
> swift as wind and rain,
> as if bursting from the earth,
> as if falling from the sky,

none can respond to or defend against it.
> Fast as bolts and arrows, how can it be matched?
> Now dark, now bright, who can know its beginning and end?

Before one has seen its launching, it invariably has already arrived.
[15/147/1–11]

15.11

Thus the one skilled in arms, on seeing the deficiency of the enemy,
>   takes advantage of it and does not rest,
>   pursues it and does not let it go,
>   presses it and does not [let it] get away.

He
>   strikes while [the enemy] is in doubt,
>   overruns him while he hesitates.

[He is like]
>   swift thunder that does not give [the enemy] time to cover his
>   ears,
>   fast lightning that leaves [the enemy] no leisure to cover his eyes.

The one skilled in arms
>   is like the sound to the echo,
>   is like the gong to the drum.
>   If a mote gets into [the enemy's] eye, he does not allow him to
>   wipe it away;
>   if [the enemy] exhales, he does not allow him to inhale.

At this time,
>   he does not look up to see Heaven;
>   he does not look down to view Earth;
>   his hand does not lift his spear;
>   his weapon is not fully drawn.
>   He strikes [the enemy] like thunder;
>   he hits him like the wind;
>   he scorches him like fire;
>   he overcomes him like a wave.

The enemy
>   does not know where to stay while at rest,
>   does not know what to do while in motion.

Thus when the drums sound and the flags wave, none facing him do not give up or collapse. Who in the world dares to display might or maintain discipline when facing him? Therefore, one who anticipates others is victorious; one who awaits others is defeated; one who is led by others dies. [15/147/11–16]

15.12

[One]

> whose soldiers are still stands firm,
> who is concentrated and united is mighty,
> whose duties are apportioned is brave,
> whose mind is in doubt flees,
> whose strength is divided is weak.

Thus, if you can divide his soldiers and cause his mind to doubt, a small fraction [of his strength] will be more than enough. If you cannot divide his soldiers and cause his mind to doubt, many times [his strength] will not suffice.

> Djou's soldiers numbered one million and had one million minds;
> King Wu's soldiers numbered three thousand and all were concentrated and united.

Thus,

> one thousand men of the same mind yield the strength of a thousand men;
> ten thousand men with different minds do not have the usefulness of one man.

When commander and soldiers, officials and people, all move and rest as if one body, you may respond to the enemy and join battle. Thus,

> [when] you set off after plans are firm,
> move after duties are apportioned,
> the commander has no doubtful designs;
> the soldiers have no separate mind;
> in motion there is no lax demeanor;
> in speech there are no empty words;
> in tasks there is no tentativeness;
> [then you] will surely respond to the enemy quickly;
> [you] will surely initiate actions swiftly.

Thus,

> the commander takes the people as his body,
> and the people take the commander as their mind.
> When the mind is sincere, the limbs and body will be close and cleave [to it];

when the mind is doubtful, the limbs and body will rebel and
flee.

If the mind is not concentrated and unified, the body will not be
disciplined in action;

if the commander is not sincere and sure, the soldiers will not be
brave and daring.

Thus the soldiers of a good commander
are like the fangs of the tiger,
like the horn of the rhinoceros,
like the wings of a bird,
like the feet of a millipede.

They can advance;
they can withdraw;
they can bite;
they can butt.

They are strong without defeating one another;
they are numerous without harming one another;

one mind moves them.

Thus,

when the people earnestly follow orders, though they are few,
there is nothing to fear;

when the people do not follow orders, though they are many, they
act as few.

Thus,

when inferiors are not close to superiors. [the commander's]
mind is of no use;

when the soldiers do not fear the commander, his formations will
not do battle.

Among defenses there are those that are sure to hold;
among attacks there are those that are sure to triumph

before weapons cross or edges meet the crux of survival and destruction has invariably formed. [15/147/18–28]

15.13

The military has three [types of] force and two [forms of] heft.[38]
>There is the force of *qi*;
>there is the force of terrain;
>there is the force of circumstance.
>When the commander is full of courage and scorns the enemy;
>when soldiers are daring and take joy in battle;

when amid the three armies and within the myriad hosts,
>their will leaps to the sky;
>their *qi* is like the whirlwind;
>their sound is like thunder.

Their sincerity amasses and their [essence][39] overflows, so that their might falls on the enemy. These are called "the force of *qi*."
>Mountain trails and marshy passes,
>great mountains and famous obstructions,
>"dragon coils," "umbrella peaks,"
>"sheep intestine paths," "fish trap gates":[40]

when one person holds the defile, one thousand men do not dare pass. These are called "the force of terrain."
Relying on their being
>belabored and fatigued, negligent and disordered,
>hungry and thirsty, frozen or scorched,
>pushing them where they are unsteady,
>squeezing them where they are spread thin,

these are called "the force of circumstance."
>Skillfully using spies,
>carefully laying plans,

---

38. The word translated here as "heft," *quan*, is a very richly multivalent term used in a technical military sense. *Quan* literally refers to the weight of a scale, and in different philosophical contexts it can mean "authority" or "expediency." In military texts and here in *Huainanzi* 15, it means the forms of advance training or preparation that can "tip the scales" on the field of battle, ergo "heft."

39. Following Wang Niansun's emendation. See Lau and Chen, *Huainanzi zhuzi suoyin*, 148n.2.

40. All four of these phrases seem to be set literary terms for types of terrain.

establishing ambushes,

concealing their form,

emerging where he does not expect, [thus] giving the enemy's soldiers no suitable defense. These are called "the heft of knowledge."

[When]

the formations of soldiers are correct,

the front rank is elite,

they advance and retreat together;

the units and squads [maintain] tight [formation];

the front and the rear do not restrain each other;

the left and the right do not interfere with each other.

[When] the blows received are few,

the enemy wounded are many;

these are called "the heft of training."

[When]

advantage and force are surely formed,

officers and soldiers are concentrated and excellent,

the able are chosen and the talented employed;

each office finds its [right] person.

[When]

plans are set and strategies decided,

death and life are clear.

[When] taking and releasing attain their [proper] time [and] none are not aroused and alert, then

before the assault [employs] the battering ram or siege ladder, the city is taken;

before in battle weapons cross or edges meet, the enemy is broken.

This is to be enlightened about the arts of certain victory.

Thus,

if arms are not sure to be victorious, one does not rashly cross blades;

if the assault is not sure to take [its object], one does not rashly launch [it].

Only after victory is certain does one give battle;

only after the scales[41] have been weighed does one move.
Thus,

> the masses form up and do not vainly scatter;
> the soldiers set out and do not fruitlessly return. [15/148/1–11]

15.14

On moving, only one who is devoid of a single movement scrapes the sky and shakes the earth.

> Lifting Mount Tai,[42]
> blocking the Four Seas,
> moving and shifting ghosts and spirits,
> alarming and startling birds and beasts,

[when] one is like this,

> in the countryside there are none who study arms;
> throughout the kingdom there are no defended cities.
> Meet agitation with stillness,
> match chaos with order,
> be without form and control what has form,
> be without purpose and respond to alterations,

though this will not yet make you able to gain victory over the enemy, it will allow the enemy no path to victory.

> When the enemy moves before me, then from this I see his form.
> When he is agitated and I am still, then with this I can obstruct his strength.
> When his form is seen, then victory may be fashioned.
> When his strength is obstructed, [my] might may be established.
> View his purposes and transform in accord with them,
> observe his deviancy and straightness and thereby control his fate,

---

41. Following commentators' reading of *ling* as *quan*. See Lau and Chen, *Huainanzi zhuzi suoyin*, 148nn.1, 10.

42. Mount Tai 泰山 is China's most sacred mountain, located in present-day Shandong Province.

feed him what he desires and thereby stop up his contentment.
If he has a fissure,

> quickly rush into the crack.
>
> Compass his alterations and bind him,
> plumb his rhythms and unbalance[43] him.
>
> If the enemy returns to stillness, produce something unexpected for him;
>
> if he does not respond, unilaterally extinguish his [sense of] security.
>
> If I move and he responds, I can see his purposes;
>
> if he holds back, push him to move him;
>
> if he has accumulated something, there must be something that he lacks.
>
> If his best troops turn left, trap his right flank;
>
> if the enemy breaks and runs, his rear may definitely be moved.

[When] the enemy is pressed and does not move, this is called "lingering."

> Strike him like thunder;
> cut him like grass or trees;
> burn him like fire or lightning.

You must hurry fast

> [so that] his men have no time to run,
> his carts have no time to roll,
> his weapons are like wooden plants,
> his crossbows are like sheep horns.

Though his men are numerous, [your] force is such that he dare not strike. [15/148/11–21]

15.15

> Of all things that have an image, there is not [one] that cannot be defeated;

---

43. Accepting Lau and Chen's (*Huainanzi zhuzi suoyin*, 148n.11) proposed emendation.

of all things that have form, there is none for which there is no
  response.
This is why the sage lodges in Nothingness and lets his mind roam in
Emptiness.
  Wind and rain can be blocked and screened,
    but cold and heat cannot be shut out;
it is because they have no form. What can suffuse the essentially
subtle,
    pierce metal and stone,
    reach the farthest distance,
    rise above the Nine Heavens,
    [and] coil below the Yellow Springs[44]
is only the Formless.
One who is skilled at using arms
    should attack [the enemy's] disorder
    [but] should not assault his order.
    Do not attack well-dressed ranks;
    do not assault upright flags.
If his demeanor cannot yet be seen, match him with equal numbers. If
he has the form of death, follow and control him. If the enemy holds
[superior] numbers, stay hidden while moving. If you meet fullness
with deficiency, you surely will be captured by him.
    If tigers and leopards did not move, they would not enter the pit.
    If deer and elk did not move, they would not be taken by nets.
    If flying birds did not move, they would not be caught in snares.
    If fish and turtles did not move, they would not be grabbed by lips
      and beaks.
  Among things there is none that is not controlled by its motion. For
this reason, the sage values stillness.
    He is still and thus can respond to agitation;
    he follows and thus can respond to one who leads;

---

44. The Yellow Springs are the traditional Chinese underworld, toward which, according
  to some traditions, the spirits of the dead descend.

he is artful and can thus defeat one who is coarse;
he is broad-reaching and can thus capture one who is deficient.
[15/148/21–15/149/5]

15.16

Thus, for the good commander's use of soldiers,
    he merges their minds;
    he unites their strength;
    the brave cannot advance alone;
    the cowardly cannot retreat alone.
    At rest like hills and mountains,
    unleashed like the wind and rain,
what they hit surely breaks; nothing is not destroyed or drenched. They move as a single body; none can respond to or defend against [them].
    The five fingers tapping in turn are not as good as the whole hand
        rolled into a fist;
    ten thousand men advancing in turn are not as good as one hun-
        dred men arriving together.
    Tigers and leopards have better speed;
    bears and grizzlies have more strength;
yet people eat their meat and make mats of their hides because they are not able to communicate their knowledge and unite their strength.[45]

The force of water overcomes fire, [but] if the Zhanghua Tower[46] caught fire, if one sought to save it by dousing it with ladles and spoons, though one emptied a well and drained a pond, it would be no use. [But] if one picked up pots, urns, bowls, and basins and drenched it, [the fire's] being extinguished would only be a matter of time.

Now humans with respect to [other] humans do not have the advantage of water over fire, and if they wish to match the many with the few,

---

45. A similar point about the advantage that humans have over animals is made in *Huai-nanzi* 19.5. See Major et al., *Huainanzi*, 777.
46. The Zhanghua Tower was a fabled tower erected by King Ling of Chu 楚靈王 (r. 540–529 B.C.E.).

they will clearly not achieve their aim. One of the military traditions has a saying: "The few can match the many." This refers to what one commands, not with which one gives battle. Some command many but use only a few, thus their force is not on a par [with their numbers]. One who commands a few but uses many [of them] increases his functional strength. If people employ their talents to the fullest and completely use their strength, it has never been heard of from antiquity to the current day that the few have defeated the many. [15/149/7–15]

15.17

There is no spirit nobler than Heaven;
there is no force more versatile than Earth;
there is no motion more swift than time;
there is no resource more advantageous than people.
These four are the pillars and trunks of the military, yet they must rely on the Way to operate because [the Way] can unite their functions.
The advantage of terrain overcomes Heaven and time;
clever tactics overcome the advantage of terrain;
force overcomes people.
Thus,
one who relies on Heaven can be led astray;
one who relies on Earth can be trapped;
one who relies on time can be pressured;
one who relies on people can be fooled.
Humaneness, courage, trustworthiness, and incorruptibility are the most excellent qualities among people. However,
the brave can be lured;
the humane can be robbed;
the trustworthy are easily cheated;
the incorruptible are easily schemed against.
If the commander of a host has even one of these [flaws], he will be taken captive. Seen from this perspective, it also is clear that victory in arms is produced by the Pattern of the Way, not by the worthiness of human character.

Thus, deer and elk can be seized by snares;
fish and turtle can be taken by nets;
geese and swans can be collected with the dart and line.
Only to the Formless may nothing be done. For this reason, the sage
lodges in the Sourceless, so his feelings cannot be grasped and
observed;
moves in the Formless, so his formations cannot be attained and
traced.
He has no model and no protocol;
he does what is appropriate [for what] arrives;
he has no name and no shape;
he fashions [a new] image for [each] change.
How deep!
How distant!
Through winter and summer,
through spring and fall,
above reaching the highest branch,
below fathoming the deepest depth,
changing and transforming,
never hesitating or halting,
he sets his mind in the Field of Profound Mystery
and lodges his will in the Spring of the Nine Returns.[47]
Though one has acute eyes, who can detect his feelings? [15/149/
15–24]

15.18

What soldiers discuss secretly is the Way of Heaven;
what they chart and draw is the terrain;
what they speak of openly is human affairs;

---

47. The provenance of this metaphor is obscure. Gao You 高誘 notes that "nine returns"
denotes a spring that is "supremely deep." Apparently, both this sobriquet and that of
the preceding line signify the Way.

what decides victory for them is heft and force.
Thus the superior commander's use of soldiers:
> Above reaches the Way of Heaven,
> below reaches the benefit of the terrain;

between [these], he reaches the minds of the people. He then moves them at the fulcral moment and launches them [replete] with force. This is why he never has broken armies or defeated soldiers.

Coming to the mediocre commander:
> Above he does not understand the Way of Heaven;
> below he does not understand the benefit of the terrain;

he exclusively uses people and force. Though he will not be perfectly [successful], his balance will mostly be victories.

About the inferior commander's use of soldiers:
> He is broadly informed yet is himself disordered;
> he has much knowledge yet doubts himself;
> at rest he is afraid;
> setting forth he hesitates.

For this reason, when he moves he becomes another's captive. [15 / 149 / 26–30]

Now let two people cross blades. If their skill or clumsiness is no different, the braver warrior will certainly win. Why is this? It is because of the sincerity of his actions. If you use a great ax on logs and firewood, you need not wait for a beneficial time or a good day to chop it. If you put the ax on top of the logs and firewood without the aid of human effort, though you accord with the "far-flight" asterism[48] and have hold of recision and accretion,[49] you will not chop it because there is no force.

Thus,
> when water is agitated, it dries up;
> when an arrow is agitated, it flies far.

---

48. For the "far-flight" asterism, see Major, *Heaven and Earth in Early Han Thought*, 218. Far-flight, at the tip of the "handle" of the Northern Dipper constellation, acts as a moving pointer that indicates the directions associated with the twelve months.

49. For this usage of *xingde*, see n. 24.

The end of an arrow made of Qiwei bamboo[50] and capped with silver and tin could not on its own pierce even a vest of thin silk or a shield of rotten leaves. If you lend it the strength of sinew and bone, the force of bow or crossbow, then it will pierce rhino[-hide] armor and pass through a leather shield!

The speed of the wind can reach the point of blowing away roofs or breaking trees, [but] if an empty carriage reaches a great thoroughfare from atop a high hill, a person has pushed it.[51] For this reason, the force of one who is skilled at using arms is

like releasing amassed water from a thousand-*ren*[-high] dike,

like rolling round stones into a ten-thousand-*zhang*[-deep] gorge.[52]

When the world sees that my soldiers will certainly be effective, then who will dare offer me battle? Thus one hundred men who are sure to die are worth more than ten thousand men who are sure to flee; how much more is the multitude of the three armies who will enter fire and water without turning tail! Even if I challenged the entire world to cross blades, who would dare step up first? [15/150/1–9]

15.19

[These are] what are called the "divisions of Heaven":

The Green Dragon to the left, the White Tiger to the right,

the Vermilion Bird in front, the Dark Warrior behind.[53]

---

50. The phrase *qiwei junlu* 淇衛箘簬 is obscure. *Junlu* clearly refers to a type of thin but durable bamboo that is well suited to making arrows. Xu Shen glosses *qiwei* as the name of a region from which (presumably very excellent) bamboo is harvested, but other commentators offer divergent readings. See Zhang, *Huainanzi jiaoshi*, 2:1602nn.14, 37.

51. Accepting Sun Yirang's proposed emendation. See Lau and Chen, *Huainanzi zhuzi suoyin*, 150n.5. The carriage in question is a two-wheel rig, which is why the force of the wind would not make it simply roll down the hill.

52. One *ren* is eight Chinese feet, and one *zhang* is ten Chinese feet. One Chinese foot (*chi*) is approximately nine inches (twenty-three centimeters). This passage roughly parallels *Sunzi* A4/476.

53. These are constellations marking the four cardinal directions; the orientation implied here is a ruler's-eye view, facing south.

What is called the "advantages of Earth"?
> Life behind and death in front,
> valleys on the left and hills on the right.

What is called "human affairs"?
> Rewards being trustworthy and punishments sure,
> movement and stillness being timely,
> withdrawal and emplacement being swift.

These are what the ages have passed down as models and signs, [and] they are venerable.[54] But they are not that by which one survives. [True] models and signs are those that change and transform in accordance with the times. Thus,

> One stands in the shade of the upper hall and knows the progress of the sun and moon;
> one sees the ice at the bottom of the jar and knows the cold and hot [seasons] of the world.

That by which things give form to one another is subtle; only the sage fathoms its utmost. Thus,

> though the drum is not among the five tones, it is the master of the five tones;[55]
> though water is not among the five flavors, it blends the five flavors;
> though the commander is not among the five officers, he controls the five officers.
> [The drum] can harmonize the five tones because it is not among the five tones;
> [water] can blend the five flavors because it is not among the five flavors;
> [the commander] can order the affairs of the five officers because he [himself] cannot be surveyed or measured.

For this reason, the mind of the commander is
> warm like the spring, hot like the summer,
> cool like the fall, cold like the winter.

---

54. Accepting Lau and Chen's (*Huainanzi zhuzi suoyin*, 150n.6) emendation.
55. This refers to the five notes of the traditional Chinese pentatonic scale. The repetition of fives in the following passage invokes the Five Phases of *qi* (fire, wood, earth, water, and metal), which were basic categories in early cosmological thought.

He
>
> accords with conditions and transforms with them,
> follows the seasons and shifts with them. [15/150/11–19]

15.20

>
> A shadow cannot be crooked if the thing [itself] is straight;
> an echo cannot be a high note if the sound [itself] is a low note.

Observe what he sends and respond to each with what defeats it. For this reason,

> hold up Rightness and move, promote order and set forth;
> conceal your nodal points, and discard your injuries;

rely on your strengths, and complete your objective. Make him

> know your coming out but not know your going in;
> know your withdrawing but not know your amassing.
> Be at first like a fox or a raccoon dog,[56]
> then he will advance at ease.
> On meeting, be like a rhino or a tiger,
> then the enemy will take flight.
> When a soaring bird strikes, it pulls in its head;
> when a ferocious beast attacks, it conceals its claws.
> The tiger and leopard do not let their fangs show;
> biting dogs do not show their teeth.

Thus the Way of using arms is to

> show them softness and meet them with hardness,
> show them weakness and ride them with strength,
> make [as if] contracting and respond to them by expanding.
> When the commander wants to go west, he shows them east.
> At first he stands aloof, yet after he engages,
> in front he is dark yet behind he is bright.

---

56. *Grand dictionnaire Ricci de la langue chinoise* (Paris: Institut Ricci, 2001), 3:1212, defines *li* 貍 as *Nyctereutes procyonoides*, commonly known as the raccoon dog and also widely known by its Japanese name, *tanuki*. It has "the appearance of a small fox-like canid with fur markings similar to those of a raccoon."

Like ghosts, leaving no tracks;
like water, bearing no scars.
Thus
where he tends toward is not where he arrives;
what he reveals is not what he plans.
Taking, giving, moving, resting, none can recognize him. Like the stroke of thunder, one cannot prepare for him. He does not repeat [any tactic] he uses, so he can always be victorious. He communicates with the Mysterious Brilliance; none knows his portals. This is known as the Supremely Spiritlike. [15/150/21–28]

15.21

What makes the military strong is being set on death.
What makes the people set on death is Rightness.
What makes Rightness able to be practiced is awesomeness.
For this reason,
gather them with civility;
order them with martiality.
This is called "sure attainment." When awesomeness and Rightness are practiced together, this is known as "supreme strength."
What people take joy in is life,
and what they hate is death.
Even so,
at high walls and deep moats,
when arrows and stones fall like rain;
on flat plains and broad marshes,
where naked blades cross and meet,
soldiers will compete to advance and engage [the enemy]. It is not that they scorn death and take joy in injury; it is because rewards are trustworthy and punishments are clear. [15/151/1–5]
For this reason,
if superiors view inferiors as sons,
inferiors will view superiors as fathers.
If superiors view inferiors as younger brothers.

inferiors will view superiors as older brothers.

If superiors view inferiors as sons, they will surely be king over the Four Seas;

if inferiors view superiors as fathers, they will surely rectify the world.

If superiors are intimate with inferiors as with younger brothers, then they will not [find it] difficult to die for [their superiors].

If inferiors see their superiors as older brothers, then they will not [find it] difficult to perish [for their inferiors].

For this reason, one cannot fight with opponents who are [as close as] fathers, sons, older brothers, and younger brothers because of the goodwill accumulated over previous generations.

Thus,

if the four horses were not in harmony, [even] Zaofu would not be able to travel far;[57]

if bow and arrow were not in harmony, [even] Yi would not be able to always hit the mark;[58]

if ruler and minister were of separate minds, [even] Sunzi would not be able to face the enemy.[59]

Thus,

within, [the ruler] cultivates his governance in accumulating Potency;

without, he stops up resentment [by causing people to] submit to his awesomeness. [15/151/6–10]

15.22

Investigate the [soldiers'] labor and ease so as to be aware of their fullness and hunger, so when the day of battle arrives, they will view death

---

57. Zaofu was a fabulously skilled charioteer of legend.

58. Yi was a great archer of legend.

59. Sunzi 孫子 (also known as Sun Wu 武) was a native of Qi and general of the state of Wu during the Spring and Autumn period. He is the putative author of the *Sunzi bingfa.*

as a homecoming. The commander must share the troops' sweetness and bitterness, matching their hunger and cold. Thus he can win their [loyalty unto] death, even to the last man.

Thus in antiquity, skillful commanders were sure to personally take the lead.

In the heat, they did not spread a canopy;
in the cold, they did not don furs,
so as to equal [the soldiers'] heat and cold.

In narrow defiles they would not ride;
going uphill they would always dismount,[60]
so as to match [the soldiers'] fatigue and ease.

When the army's food was cooked, only then did they dare eat;
when the army's well had been bored, only then did they dare drink,
so as to share [the soldiers'] hunger and thirst.

When battle was joined, they would stand where the arrows and stones were arriving, so as to partake of [the soldiers'] safety and danger.

Thus the good commander's use of soldiers constantly
struck accumulated resentment with accumulated Potency,
struck accumulated hatred with accumulated love.

Why would he not triumph? [15/151/10–15]

What the ruler asks of the people is twofold:

He asks the people to labor for him;
he wants the people to die for him.

What the people hope of the ruler is threefold:

That if they are hungry, he will feed them;
that if they are fatigued, he will rest them;
that if they have merit, he will be able to reward them.

If the people fulfill their two duties and the ruler disappoints their three hopes, though the kingdom is large and the people numerous, the military will be weak.

The embittered must attain what they take joy in;
the belabored must attain what they find profit in.

---

60. Accepting Wang Shumin's emendation. See Lau and Chen, *Huainanzi zhuzi suoyin*, 15n.9A. The reference is probably to dismounting from a chariot, not from riding astride.

The merit of "cutting heads" must be fully [remunerated];
service unto death must be posthumously rewarded.
If in these four, one keeps faith with the people, even if the ruler
shoots at birds in the clouds, angles for fish in the deep abyss,
plucks the *qin* and *se*, listens to bells and pipes,[61]
plays *liubo* or tosses "high pots,"[62]
the military will still be strong;
orders will still be carried out.
For this reason, if superiors are worthy of reverence, inferiors may be
used; if one's Potency is worthy of admiration, one's awesomeness may
be established. [15/151/17–22]

15.23

The commander must have three guides, four ethics, five practices,
and ten disciplines.
What are called the three guides
above understand the Way of Heaven,
below study the shape of the terrain,
among them investigate the feelings of the people.
What are called the four ethics

---

61. The *qin* 琴, commonly but misleadingly translated as "lute," was a stringed instrument that in the Warring States and Han periods had a wooden sounding board attached to a thinner neck, with five to ten strings secured to the top of the neck and stretched over a wide bridge on the sounding board, beyond which they were attached to individual tuning pegs. As the *qin* later evolved in the post-Han period, the "neck" eventually disappeared, and the instrument consisted of the sounding board only, tapering from a wider end to a narrower one.

The *se* 瑟, sometimes translated as "zither," was a stringed instrument with a wide, hollow wooden sounding board and (usually) twenty-five strings that passed over fixed bridges at each end of the sounding board and were secured by pegs. The instrument was tuned by means of individual movable bridges. The *se* was popular in ancient China but fell into neglect after the Han period.

62. *Liubo* was a board game, played for gambling stakes and used as a form of divination. An anecdote involving a chesslike game, possibly *liubo*, appears in *Huainanzi* 18.27. See Major et al., *Huainanzi*, 753–54. "Tossing pots" was also a popular game.

benefit the kingdom without favoring the military,
serve the ruler without thought for themselves,
face difficulty without fearing death,
decide doubts without avoiding punishment.
What are called the five conducts
are soft but unable to be rolled up,
are hard but unable to be snapped,
are humane but unable to be insulted,
are faithful but unable to be cheated,
are brave but unable to be overcome.
What are called the ten disciplines?
Your spirit is pure and cannot be sullied;
your plans are far-reaching and cannot be anticipated;
your training is firm and cannot be moved;
your awareness is lucid and cannot be blocked;
you are not greedy[63] for wealth;
you are not corrupted by things;
you are not taken in by disputation;
you are not moved by [occult] arts;
you cannot be pleased;
you cannot be angered.
This is called the perfect model. Obscure! Mysterious! Who understands his feelings? [The ideal commander's] initiatives surely accord with the heft;[64]
his words surely correspond to the measure;
his actions surely comply with the seasons;
his resolutions surely hit the [correct] pattern.
he comprehends the activation of motion and stillness;
he is enlightened to the rhythm of opening and closing;
he has investigated the benefit and harm of removing and deploying,
so that [they are] as if merging two halves of a tally.
He is swift like a cocked crossbow;

---

63. Following the reading in Zhang, *Huainanzi jiaoshi*, 2:1613, of *tan* 貪 in place of *shi* 食.
64. Accepting Lau and Chen's (*Huainanzi zhuzi suoyin*, 151n.12) emendation of the character *quan*: 權, not 詮.

his force is like that of a released arrow,
Now a dragon, now a snake;
his movements have no constant shape.
None sees his middle;
none know his end.
When he attacks, there is no defense;
when he defends, he cannot be attacked. [15/151/24–15/152/2]

It has been said that one who is skilled at the use of arms must first cultivate it in himself [and] only afterward seek it in other people. He must first make himself invincible and only then seek out victory.

To [look for] self-cultivation from others and beg victory from the enemy, not yet being able to order oneself and yet attacking another's disorder; these are like

extinguishing fire with [more] fire,
responding to a flood with [more] water.

What can it accomplish?

Now if a potter were to be transformed into clay, he could not
fashion plates and pots.
If a weaver girl were to be transformed into silk, she could not
weave patterned cloth.

Like [things] do not suffice to control one another, thus only [something] different can be extraordinary. If two sparrows are fighting with each other, the arrival of a falcon or a hawk will break them apart because they are of a different sort.

Thus stillness is extraordinary to agitation, [and] order is extraordinary to chaos;
fullness is extraordinary to hunger, [and] ease is extraordinary to labor.

The mutual response of the extraordinary and the usual are like [the way that] water, fire, metal, and wood take turns being servant and master.

The one who is skilled at the use of arms maintains the five lethal [conducts] in responding, so he can complete his victory. The one who is clumsy abides in the five fatal [flaws] and is avaricious, so when he moves he becomes another's captive.[65] [15/152/4–9]

---

65. This appears to refer to the "five conducts" (and the matched "five failings") listed earlier as aspects of the ideal commander.

15.24

The military values plans being unfathomable and formations being concealed. Emerge where one is not expected, so [the enemy] cannot prepare a defense.

If plans are seen, they will fail;
if formations are seen, they will be controlled.

Thus one who is skilled at using arms,

above hides them in Heaven,
below hides them in Earth,
between hides them among people.

One who hides them in Heaven can control anything. What is called "hiding them in Heaven"? It is to transform in accordance with

great cold, profound heat,
swift wind, violent rain,
heavy fog, or dark night.

What is called "hiding it in Earth"? It is being able to conceal one's formations amid

mountains, hills,
forests, and valleys.

What is called "hiding it among people"?

Blocking their view in front,
facing them in the rear.

While producing an unexpected [maneuver] or moving a formation,

breaking forth like thunder,
rushing like the wind and rain.

Furling the great banners, silencing the loud drums so that one's coming and going has no traces; none knows their beginning or end. [15/152/11–15]

When front and rear are correctly aligned, the four corners are as if bound together;

when coming and going, disengaging and continuing do not interfere with one another;

when light [troops] are at the wings and crack [soldiers] are at the flanks, some forward and some at the rear;

when in parting and merging, dispersing and concentrating, companies and squads are not broken up;

this is to be skilled at deploying moving formations.

When one is clear as to freak occurrences and anomalies, yin and yang, recision and accretion, the Five Phases, the observance of *qi*, astrology,[66] and spirit supplication,[67] this is to be skillful at the Way of Heaven.

When one establishes plans, places ambushes,
uses fire and water,[68] produces anomalies.

When one has the army shout and drum so as to confuse [the enemy's] ears and drags bundled sticks to kick up dust and confuse [the enemy's] eyes; all these are being skilled at deception and dissimulation.

When the *chun*[69] sounds resolutely,
when one's will is firm[70] and not easily frightened,
when one cannot be lured by force or advantage,
when one cannot be shaken by death or defeat,

these are to be skilled at bolstering strength.

When one is agile and quick to strike,
when one is brave and scorns the enemy,
when one is swift as [a horse at] the gallop,

these are to be skilled at using speed and creating surprise.

When one assesses the shape of the terrain,
lodges at rest camps,
fixes walls and fortifications,
is careful of depressions[71] and salt marshes,
occupies the high ground,

---

66. These all are cosmological categories and forms of divination used to forecast battle-field conditions. Observing *qi* is a form of military prognostication by means of which one ascertains victory or defeat by surveying the *qi* emanating from the enemy army. It is described in *Mozi* 68.

67. That is, rituals and prayers used to solicit the aid of the spirit world.

68. The character *jian* here is a superfluous intrusion into the text. See Lau and Chen, *Huainanzi zhuzi suoyin*, 152n.2.

69. The *chun* is a hollow bronze musical instrument shaped like an inverted pear and played by striking.

70. Reading *zhi* as "will." See Zhang, *Huainanzi jiaoshi*, 2:1620n.8.

71. Reading *yan* 煙 as having a water radical on the left: 湮. See Sun Yirang's proposed emendation in Lau and Chen, *Huainanzi zhuzi suoyin*, 152n.4.

avoids exposed positions,
these are to be skilled at using the shape of the terrain.
When one relies on [the enemy's] hunger, thirst, cold and heat,
when one belabors his fatigue and aggravates his disorder,
when one deepens his fear and hampers his steps,
when one hits him with elite troops,
when one strikes him at night,
these are to be skilled at according with the seasons and responding to change.
[When one] uses chariots on easy [terrain],
mounted horsemen on obstructed [terrain],
[when one] uses more bowmen while crossing water,
uses more crossbowmen in a narrow pass,
[when one] uses more flags by day,
uses more fires by night,
uses more drums at dusk,
these are to be skilled in logistics.
One cannot lack even one of these eight, even though they are not what is most valuable to the military. [15/152/17–26]

15.25

The commander must see singularly and know singularly.
Seeing singularly is to see what is not seen.
Knowing singularly is to know what is not known.
To see what others do not is called "enlightenment."
To know what others do not is called "spiritlike."
The spiritlike and enlightened is one who triumphs in advance. He who triumphs in advance
cannot be attacked when he defends,
cannot be defeated in battle,
cannot be defended against when he attacks.
This is because of emptiness and fullness.
When there is a gap between superiors and inferiors, when the commander and officials do not cooperate, when what one

upholds is not straight, when the minds of the soldiers accumulate insubordination, this is called "emptiness."

When the ruler is enlightened and the commander competent,
when superiors and inferiors are of the same mind, when [the
soldiers'] *qi* and intentions both are aroused, this is called "fullness."

It is like throwing water at fire:

What it lands on squarely will collapse;
what it hits sparsely will be moved.
Hard and soft do not interpenetrate,
victory and defeat[72] are alien to each other.

This speaks of emptiness and fullness.

Being skilled at battle does not reside in the few;
being skilled at defense does not reside in the small;
victory resides in attaining awesomeness;
defeat resides in losing *qi*. [15/153/1–4]
The full should fight, the empty should run;
the thriving should be strong, the declining should flee.

The territory of King Fuchai of Wu was two thousand *li* square, and
he had seventy thousand armored warriors.[73]

To the south he fought with Yue and routed them at Kuaiji.
To the north he fought with Qi and broke them at Ailing.
To the west he met the Duke of Jin and captured him at Huang-
chi.[74]

This is to use the people's *qi* when it is full. Afterward

he became arrogant and gave free rein to his desires;
he scorned admonition and took delight in slander;
he was violent and followed erroneous [advice];

---

72. Following Yang Shuda's proposed emendation. See Lau and Chen, *Huainanzi zhuzi suoyin*, 153n.3.

73. King Fuchai 夫差 (r. 495–477 B.C.E.) was the ruler of Wu, a non-Chinese kingdom in the Lower Yangtze region. His struggle with his arch rival, King Goujian 勾踐 of Yue (r. 496–465 B.C.E.), is the subject of much romantic prose.

74. The battle at Kuaiji occurred in 494 B.C.E., that at Ailing in 489 B.C.E., and that at Huangchi in 482 B.C.E.

he could not be spoken to honestly.
> The great officials were resentful;
> the people were insubordinate.

The king of Yue and three thousand elite troops captured [Fuchai] at Gansui.[75] This was taking advantage of his emptiness.

That *qi* has empty and full [phases] is like the darkness following the light. Thus,

> a victorious military is not always full;
> a defeated military is not always empty.
> He who is skilled can fill his people's *qi* while awaiting others' emptiness.
> He who is incapable empties his people's *qi* while awaiting others' fullness.

Thus the *qi* of emptiness and fullness are what is most valued by the military. [15/153/6–11]

15.26

Whenever the kingdom has difficulty, from the palace the ruler summons the commander, charging him: "The fate of the altars of the soil and grain are on your person. The kingdom faces a crisis, I wish you to take command and respond to it."

When the commander has accepted his mandate, [the ruler] orders the Supplicator and Great Diviner to fast, sequestered for three days. Going to the Great Temple, they consult the Magic Tortoise to divine a lucky day for receiving the drums and flags.

The ruler enters the temple portal, faces west, and stands. The commander enters the temple portal, rushes to the foot of the platform, faces north, and stands.

The sovereign personally grasps the *yue* ax. Holding it by the head, he offers the commander its handle, saying, "From here up to Heaven is controlled by [you,] the commander." [The ruler] again grasps the

---

75. Fuchai's final defeat at the hands of Yue occurred in 473 B.C.E.

fu ax. Holding it by the head, he offers the commander its handle, saying, "From here down to the Abyss is controlled by [you,] the commander."[76]

    When the commander has accepted the *fu* and *yue* axes, he replies,
      "[Just as] the kingdom cannot be governed from without,
      the army cannot be ruled from within.[77]
      [Just as] one cannot serve the ruler with two minds,
      one cannot respond to the enemy with a doubtful will.

Since [I,] your minister, have received control from you, I exclusively [wield] the authority of the drums, flags, and *fu* and *yue* axes. I ask nothing in return. I [only] hope that Your Highness likewise not hand down one word of command to me.

      If Your Highness does not agree, I dare not take command.
      If Your Highness agrees, I will take my leave and set out."

[The commander] then trims his fingernails,[78] dons funeral garb, and exits through the "ill-augured" portal.[79] He mounts the commander's chariot and arrays the banners and axes, tied as if not [yet] victorious. On meeting the enemy and committing to battle,
      he pays no heed to certain death;
      he does not have two minds.
For this reason,
      he has no Heaven above;
      he has no Earth below;
      he has no enemy in front;
      he has no ruler behind;
      he does not seek fame in advancing;
      he does not avoid punishment in retreating;

---

76. The *yue* 鉞 and *fu* 斧 axes are military regalia of the ruler. The conferring of these symbols on the commander represents the transfer of sovereign authority to him for the duration of the campaign.

77. Here "within" is used with the meaning of "within the king's court."

78. Following Yang Shuda (although retaining the original order of the text). See Lau and Chen, *Huainanzi zhuzi suoyin*, 153n.5.

79. These all are rituals demonstrating the commander's resolve to die. The "ill-augured" portal is the north portal.

he [seeks] only to protect the people;
his benefit is united with that of the ruler.

This is the treasure of the kingdom, the Way of the superior commander.

If he is like this,
the clever will plan for him;
the brave will fight for him;
their *qi* will scrape the azure clouds;
they will be swift as galloping [steeds].

Thus before weapons have clashed, the enemy is terrified.[80]

If the battle is victorious and the enemy flees, [the commander] thoroughly dispenses rewards for merit. He reassigns his officers, increasing their rank and emolument. He sets aside land and apportions it, making sure it is outside the feudal mound.[81] Last, he judges punishments within the army.

Turning back, he returns to the kingdom, lowering his banners and storing the *fu* and *yue* axes. He makes his final report to the ruler, saying, "I have no further control over the army." He then dons coarse silk and enters seclusion.

[The commander goes] to ask pardon of the ruler. The ruler says, "Spare him." [The commander] withdraws and dons fasting garb. For a great victory, he remains secluded for three years; for a middling victory, two years; for a lesser victory, one year.

That against which the military was used was surely a kingdom without the Way. Thus
one can triumph in battle without retribution,
take territory without returning it;
the people will not suffer illness;

---

80. Down to this point, the text of section 15.26 is closely paralleled by a passage in the fourth chapter of the *Taigong liutao* (*Six Secret Teachings of the Grand Duke*). See Ralph D. Sawyer, trans., *The Seven Military Classics of Ancient China* (Boulder, Colo.: Westview Press, 1993), 64–65.

81. In other words, the commander makes sure that all lands dispensed as rewards fall outside the sacred ground used for the ancestral cult of the defeated sovereign, so that sacrifices to the ancestors of the defeated line may be continued.

the commander will not die early;
the five grains will flourish;
the winds and rains will be seasonable;
the battle is won without;
good fortune is born within.

Thus one's reputation will be made, and afterward there will be no further harm. [15/153/13–29]

BIBLIOGRAPHY

Ames, Roger. *The Art of Rulership: A Study in Ancient Chinese Political Thought.* Honolulu: University of Hawai'i Press, 1983.

———, trans. *Sun-tzu: The Art of Warfare.* New York: Ballantine Books, 1993.

Ban Gu 班固. *Han shu* 漢書. Beijing: Zhonghua shuju, 1962.

Bodde, Derk. "The State and Empire of Ch'in." In *The Cambridge History of China*, vol. 1, *The Ch'in and Han Empires, 221 B.C.–A.D. 220*, edited by Denis Twitchett and Michael Loewe, 20–102. Cambridge: Cambridge University Press, 1986.

Bokenkamp, Stephen, trans. *Early Daoist Scriptures.* Berkeley: University of California Press, 1996.

Chin, Annping. *The Authentic Confucius: A Life of Thought and Politics.* New York: Scribner, 2007.

Confucius. *The Analects.* Translated by D. C. Lau. Harmondsworth: Penguin, 1979.

Cook, Constance. "Wealth and the Western Zhou." *Bulletin of the School of Oriental and African Studies* 60, no. 2 (1997): 253–94.

Creel, Herrlee G. *The Origins of Statecraft in China.* Chicago: University of Chicago Press, 1970.

———. *What Is Taoism? and Other Studies in Chinese Cultural History.* Chicago: University of Chicago Press, 1970.

Csikszentmihalyi, Mark, and Michael Nylan. "Constructing Lineages and Inventing Traditions Through Exemplary Figures in Early China," *T'oung pao* 89 (2003): 59–99.

Denecke, Wiebke. *The Dynamics of Masters Literature: Early Chinese Thought from Confucius to Han Feizi.* Cambridge, Mass.: Harvard University Asia Center, 2011.

DeWoskin, Kenneth J. *Doctors, Diviners, and Magicians of Ancient China: Biographies of Fang-shih.* New York: Columbia University Press, 1983.

Eno, Robert. *The Confucian Creation of Heaven: Philosophy and the Defense of Ritual Mastery.* Albany: State University of New York Press, 1990.

Gu Yanwu 顧炎武. *Gu Tinglin shiwen ji* 顧亭林詩文集. Beijing: Zhonghua shuju, 1983.

Henderson, John B. *The Development and Decline of Chinese Cosmology.* New York: Columbia University Press, 1984.

Johnson, David. "Epic and History in Early China: The Matter of Wu Tzu-hsü." *Journal of Asian Studies* 40, no. 2 (1981): 255–71.

——. "The Wu Tzu-hsü *Pien-wen* and Its Sources: Part I, Part II." *Harvard Journal of Asiatic Studies* 40, nos. 1–2 (1980): 93–156, 465–505.

Johnston, Ian, trans. *The Mozi: A Complete Translation.* New York: Columbia University Press, 2010.

Jullien, François. *The Propensity of Things: Toward a History of Efficacy in China.* Translated by Janet Lloyd. New York: Zone Books, 1999.

Knoblock, John, trans. *Xunzi: A Translation and Study of the Complete Works.* Vol. 2. Stanford, Calif.: Stanford University Press, 1990.

Knoblock, John, and Jeffrey Riegel, trans. *The Annals of Lü Buwei: A Complete Translation and Study.* Stanford, Calif.: Stanford University Press, 2000.

Koestler, Arthur. *Janus: A Summing Up.* New York: Random House, 1978.

Kohn, Livia, ed. *Taoist Meditation and Longevity Techniques.* Ann Arbor: Center for Chinese Studies, University of Michigan, 1989.

LaFargue, Michael, trans. *The Tao of the Tao Te Ching: A Translation and Commentary.* Albany: State University of New York Press, 1992.

Lau, D. C., trans. *Mencius.* London: Penguin, 1970.

Lau, D. C. 劉段爵, and Chen Fong Ching 陳方正, eds. *Bingshu sizhong zhuzi suoyin* 兵書四種逐字索引. Institute of Chinese Studies Ancient Chinese Text Concordance Series. Hong Kong: Commercial Press, 1992.

——. *Chunqiu Zuo zhuan zhuzi suoyin* 春秋左傳逐字索引. Institute of Chinese Studies Ancient Chinese Text Concordance Series. Hong Kong: Commercial Press, 1995.

——. *Guanzi zhuzi suoyin* 管子逐字索引. Institute of Chinese Studies Ancient Chinese Text Concordance Series. Hong Kong: Commercial Press, 2001.

——. *Hanshi waizhuan zhuzi suoyin* 韓詩外傳逐字索引. Institute of Chinese Studies Ancient Chinese Text Concordance Series. Hong Kong: Commercial Press, 1992.

——. *Huainanzi zhuzi suoyin* 淮南子逐字索引. Institute of Chinese Studies Ancient Chinese Text Concordance Series. Hong Kong: Commercial Press, 1992.

———. *Lun yu zhuzi suoyin* 論語逐字索引. Institute of Chinese Studies Ancient Chinese Text Concordance Series. Hong Kong: Commercial Press, 2006.

———. *Lüshi chunqiu zhuzi suoyin* 呂氏春秋逐字索引. Institute of Chinese Studies Ancient Chinese Text Concordance Series. Hong Kong: Commercial Press, 1994.

———. *Mengzi zhuzi suoyin* 孟子逐字索引. Institute of Chinese Studies Ancient Chinese Text Concordance Series. Hong Kong: Commercial Press, 1995.

———. *Mozi zhuzi suoyin* 墨子逐字索引. Institute of Chinese Studies Ancient Chinese Text Concordance Series. Hong Kong: Commercial Press, 2001.

———. *Zhanguoce zhuzi suoyin* 戰國策逐字索引. Institute of Chinese Studies Ancient Chinese Text Concordance Series. Hong Kong: Commercial Press, 1992.

———. *Zhuangzi zhuzi suoyin* 莊子逐字索引. Institute of Chinese Studies Ancient Chinese Text Concordance Series. Hong Kong: Commercial Press, 2000.

Le Blanc, Charles. *Huai-nan Tzu: Philosophical Synthesis in Early Han Thought; The Idea of Resonance (Kan-ying) with a Translation and Analysis of Chapter Six*. Hong Kong: Hong Kong University Press, 1985.

Lewis, Mark Edward. *Sanctioned Violence in Early China*. Albany: State University of New York Press, 1990.

———. "Warring States: Political History." In *The Cambridge History of Ancient China: From the Origins of Civilization to 221 B.C.*, edited by Michael Loewe and Edward L. Shaughnessy, 587–650. Cambridge: Cambridge University Press, 1999.

———. *Writing and Authority in Early China*. Albany: State University of New York Press, 1999.

Li Feng. *Bureaucracy and the State in Early China: Governing the Western Zhou*. Cambridge: Cambridge University Press, 2008.

———. *Landscape and Power in Early China: The Crisis and Fall of the Western Zhou, 1045–771 B.C.* Cambridge: Cambridge University Press, 2006.

Liu, James J. Y. *The Chinese Knight-Errant*. Chicago: University of Chicago Press, 1967.

Loewe, Michael. *Crisis and Conflict in Han China*. London: Allen & Unwin, 1974.

———. "The Former Han." In *The Cambridge History of China*, vol. 1, *The Ch'in and Han Empires, 221 B.C.–A.D. 220*, edited by Denis Twitchett and Michael Loewe, 103–222. Cambridge: Cambridge University Press, 1986.

———. *The Government of the Qin and Han Empires: 221 B.C.E.–220 C.E.* Indianapolis: Hackett, 2006.

Mair, Victor H. *The Art of War: Sun Zi's Military Methods*. New York: Columbia University Press, 2007.

——. *Soldierly Methods: Vade Mecum for an Iconoclastic Translation of Sun Zi bingfa*. Sino-Platonic Papers, no. 178. Philadelphia: Department of East Asian Languages and Civilizations, University of Pennsylvania, 2008.

Major, John S. *Heaven and Earth in Early Han Thought: Chapters Three, Four, and Five of the Huainanzi*. Albany: State University of New York Press, 1993.

Major, John S., and Constance Cook, eds. *Defining Chu: Image and Reality in Ancient Chin*. Honolulu: University of Hawai'i Press, 1999.

Major, John S., Sarah A. Queen, Andrew Seth Meyer, and Harold D. Roth, trans. *The Huainanzi: A Guide to the Theory and Practice of Government in Early Han China*. New York: Columbia University Press, 2010.

Mawangdui Hanmu boshu zhengli xiaozu 馬王堆漢墓帛書整理小組. *Mawang-dui Hanmu boshu* 馬王堆漢墓帛書. Beijing: Wenwu, 1980.

McMullen, David. *State and Scholars in T'ang China*. Cambridge: Cambridge University Press, 1988.

Meyer, Andrew. "'The Altars of the Soil and Grain Are Closer Than Kin': The Qi Model of Intellectual Participation and the Jixia Patronage Community." *Early China* 33 (forthcoming).

——. "Root–Branches Structuralism in the *Huainanzi*." In *Text in Context: New Perspectives on the Huainanzi*, edited by Sarah Queen and Michael Puett. Leiden: Brill, forthcoming.

Meyer, Andrew, and Andrew Wilson. "Inventing the General: A Reappraisal of the *Sunzi bingfa*." In *War, Virtual War, and Society: The Challenge to Communities*, edited by Andrew Wilson and Mark L. Perry, 151–68. Amsterdam: Rodopi, 2008.

——. "*Sunzi bingfa* as History and Theory." In *Strategic Logic and Political Rationality: Essays in Honor of Michael I. Handel*, edited by Bradford A. Lee and Karl F. Walling, 95–113. London: Cass, 2003.

Nienhauser, William H., ed. *The Grand Scribe's Records*. Vol. 7, *The Memoirs of Pre-Han China*. Bloomington: Indiana University Press, 1995.

——. *The Grand Scribe's Records*. Vol. 8, *The Memoirs of Han China*, Part 1. Bloomington: Indiana University Press, 2008.

Puett, Michael. *The Ambivalence of Creation: Debates Concerning Innovation and Artifice in Early China*. Stanford, Calif.: Stanford University Press, 2001.

——. "The Ethics of Responding Properly: The Notion of Qing in Early Chinese Thought." In *Love and Emotions in Traditional Chinese Literature*, edited by Halvor Eifring, 37–68. Leiden: Brill, 2004.

Rickett, W. Allyn, trans. *Guanzi: Political, Economic, and Philosophical Essays from Early China*. Vol. 1. Princeton, N.J.: Princeton University Press, 1985.

Roth, Harold D. "Psychology and Self-Cultivation in Early Taoistic Thought." *Harvard Journal of Asiatic Studies* 51, no. 2 (1991): 599–650.

Ryden, Edmund. *Philosophy of Peace in Han China: A Study of the Huainanzi Ch. 15 "On Military Strategy."* Taipei: Taipei Ricci Institute, 1998.

Sailey, Jay. *The Master Who Embraces Simplicity: A Study of the Philosopher Ko Hung, A.D. 283–343*. San Francisco: Chinese Materials Center, 1978.

Sawyer, Ralph. "Martial Prognostication." In *Military Culture in Imperial China*, edited by Nicola Di Cosmo, 45–64. Cambridge, Mass.: Harvard University Press, 2009.

——, trans. *The Seven Military Classics of Ancient China*. Boulder, Colo.: Westview Press, 1993.

Schwartz, Benjamin I. *The World of Thought in Ancient China*. Cambridge, Mass.: Harvard University Press, 1985.

Shaughnessy, Edward L. "'New' Evidence of the Zhou Conquest." In *Before Confucius: Studies in the Creation of the Chinese Classics*, 31–68. Albany: State University of New York Press, 1997.

——. "Western Zhou History." In *The Cambridge History of Ancient China: From the Origins of Civilization to 221 B.C.*, edited by Michael Loewe and Edward L. Shaughnessy, 292–351. Cambridge: Cambridge University Press, 1999.

Sima Qian 司馬遷. *Shi ji* 史記. Beijing: Zhonghua shuju, 1959.

Sivin, Nathan. "On the Word 'Taoism' as a Source of Perplexity: With Special Reference to the Relations of Science and Religion in Traditional China." *History of Religions* 17 (1978): 303–30.

Smith, Kidder. "Sima Tan and the Invention of Daoism, 'Legalism,' et cetera." *Journal of Asian Studies* 62, no. 1 (2003): 129–56.

Strickmann, Michel. "On the Alchemy of T'ao Hung-ching." In *Facets of Taoism: Essays in Chinese Religion*, edited by Holmes Welch and Anna Seidel, 123–92. New Haven, Conn.: Yale University Press, 1979.

Su Yu 蘇輿. *Chunqiu fanlu yizheng* 春秋繁露義證. Beijing: Zhonghua shuju, 1992.

Thompson, Paul M. *The Shen Tzu Fragments*. Oxford: Oxford University Press, 1979.

Tu Wei-ming. *Centrality and Commonality: An Essay on Confucian Religiousness*. Albany: State University of New York Press, 1989.

Vankeerberghen, Griet. *The Huainanzi and Liu An's Claim to Moral Authority*. Albany: State University of New York Press, 2001.

Wang Liqi 王利器. *Yan tie lun jiaozhu* 鹽鐵論校注. Beijing: Zhonghua shuju, 1992.

Watson, Burton, trans. *Han Fei Tzu: Basic Writings*. New York: Columbia University Press, 1964.

——, trans. *Records of the Grand Historian: Han Dynasty II*. Rev. ed. New York: Columbia University Press, 1993.

Yates, Robin D. S. "Law and the Military in Early China." In *Military Culture in Imperial China*, edited by Nicola Di Cosmo, 23–44. Cambridge, Mass.: Harvard University Press, 2009.

——. "New Light on Ancient Chinese Military Texts: Notes on Their Nature and Evolution, and the Development of Military Specialization in Warring States China." *T'oung pao* 74 (1988): 211–48.

Zhang Shuangdi 張雙棣. *Huainanzi jiaoshi* 淮南子校释. Beijing: Beijing University Press, 1997.

INDEX

Major Plays of Chikamatsu, tr. Donald Keene 1961
Four Major Plays of Chikamatsu, tr. Donald Keene. Paperback ed. only. 1961; rev. ed. 1997
Records of the Grand Historian of China, translated from the Shih chi of Ssu-ma Ch'ien, tr. Burton Watson, 2 vols. 1961
Instructions for Practical Living and Other Neo-Confucian Writings by Wang Yang-ming, tr. Wing-tsit Chan 1963
Hsün Tzu: Basic Writings, tr. Burton Watson, paperback ed. only. 1963; rev. ed. 1996
Chuang Tzu: Basic Writings, tr. Burton Watson, paperback ed. only. 1964; rev. ed. 1996
The Mahābhārata, tr. Chakravarthi V. Narasimhan. Also in paperback ed. 1965; rev. ed. 1997
The Manyōshū, Nippon Gakujutsu Shinkōkai edition 1965
Su Tung-p'o: Selections from a Sung Dynasty Poet, tr. Burton Watson. Also in paperback ed. 1965
Bhartrihari: Poems, tr. Barbara Stoler Miller. Also in paperback ed. 1967
Basic Writings of Mo Tzu, Hsün Tzu, and Han Fei Tzu, tr. Burton Watson. Also in separate paperback eds. 1967
The Awakening of Faith, Attributed to Aśvaghosha, tr. Yoshito S. Hakeda. Also in paperback ed. 1967
Reflections on Things at Hand: The Neo-Confucian Anthology, comp. Chu Hsi and Lü Tsu-ch'ien, tr. Wing-tsit Chan 1967
The Platform Sutra of the Sixth Patriarch, tr. Philip B. Yampolsky. Also in paperback ed. 1967
Essays in Idleness: The Tsurezuregusa of Kenkō, tr. Donald Keene. Also in paperback ed. 1967
The Pillow Book of Sei Shōnagon, tr. Ivan Morris, 2 vols. 1967
Two Plays of Ancient India: The Little Clay Cart and the Minister's Seal, tr. J. A. B. van Buitenen 1968
The Complete Works of Chuang Tzu, tr. Burton Watson 1968
The Romance of the Western Chamber (Hsi Hsiang chi), tr. S. I. Hsiung. Also in paperback ed. 1968
The Manyōshū, Nippon Gakujutsu Shinkōkai edition. Paperback ed. only. 1969
Records of the Historian: Chapters from the Shih chi of Ssu-ma Ch'ien, tr. Burton Watson. Paperback ed. only. 1969
Cold Mountain: 100 Poems by the T'ang Poet Han-shan, tr. Burton Watson. Also in paperback ed. 1970

Twenty Plays of the Nō Theatre, ed. Donald Keene. Also in paperback ed. 1970
Chūshingura: The Treasury of Loyal Retainers, tr. Donald Keene. Also in paperback ed. 1971; rev. ed. 1997
The Zen Master Hakuin: Selected Writings, tr. Philip B. Yampolsky 1971
Chinese Rhyme-Prose: Poems in the Fu Form from the Han and Six Dynasties Periods, tr. Burton Watson. Also in paperback ed. 1971
Kūkai: Major Works, tr. Yoshito S. Hakeda. Also in paperback ed. 1972
The Old Man Who Does as He Pleases: Selections from the Poetry and Prose of Lu Yu, tr. Burton Watson 1973
The Lion's Roar of Queen Śrīmālā, tr. Alex and Hideko Wayman 1974
Courtier and Commoner in Ancient China: Selections from the History of the Former Han by Pan Ku, tr. Burton Watson. Also in paperback ed. 1974
Japanese Literature in Chinese, vol. 1: Poetry and Prose in Chinese by Japanese Writers of the Early Period, tr. Burton Watson 1975
Japanese Literature in Chinese, vol. 2: Poetry and Prose in Chinese by Japanese Writers of the Later Period, tr. Burton Watson 1976
Love Song of the Dark Lord: Jayadeva's Gītagovinda, tr. Barbara Stoler Miller. Also in paperback ed. Cloth ed. includes critical text of the Sanskrit. 1977; rev. ed. 1997
Ryōkan: Zen Monk-Poet of Japan, tr. Burton Watson 1977
Calming the Mind and Discerning the Real: From the Lam rim chen mo of Tsoṇ-kha-pa, tr. Alex Wayman 1978
The Hermit and the Love-Thief: Sanskrit Poems of Bhartrihari and Bilhaṇa, tr. Barbara Stoler Miller 1978
The Lute: Kao Ming's P'i-p'a chi, tr. Jean Mulligan. Also in paperback ed. 1980
A Chronicle of Gods and Sovereigns: Jinnō Shōtōki of Kitabatake Chikafusa, tr. H. Paul Varley 1980
Among the Flowers: The Hua-chien chi, tr. Lois Fusek 1982
Grass Hill: Poems and Prose by the Japanese Monk Gensei, tr. Burton Watson 1983
Doctors, Diviners, and Magicians of Ancient China: Biographies of Fang-shih, tr. Kenneth J. DeWoskin. Also in paperback ed. 1983

Theater of Memory: The Plays of Kālidāsa, ed. Barbara Stoler Miller. Also in paperback ed. 1984

The Columbia Book of Chinese Poetry: From Early Times to the Thirteenth Century, ed. and tr. Burton Watson. Also in paperback ed. 1984

Poems of Love and War: From the Eight Anthologies and the Ten Long Poems of Classical Tamil, tr. A. K. Ramanujan. Also in paperback ed. 1985

The Bhagavad Gita: Krishna's Counsel in Time of War, tr. Barbara Stoler Miller 1986

The Columbia Book of Later Chinese Poetry, ed. and tr. Jonathan Chaves. Also in paperback ed. 1986

The Tso Chuan: Selections from China's Oldest Narrative History, tr. Burton Watson 1989

Waiting for the Wind: Thirty-six Poets of Japan's Late Medieval Age, tr. Steven Carter 1989

Selected Writings of Nichiren, ed. Philip B. Yampolsky 1990

Saigyō, Poems of a Mountain Home, tr. Burton Watson 1990

The Book of Lieh Tzu: A Classic of the Tao, tr. A. C. Graham. Morningside ed. 1990

The Tale of an Anklet: An Epic of South India— The Cilappatikāram of Iḷaṅkō Aṭika;dul, tr. R. Parthasarathy 1993

Waiting for the Dawn: A Plan for the Prince, tr. with introduction by Wm. Theodore de Bary 1993

Yoshitsune and the Thousand Cherry Trees: A Masterpiece of the Eighteenth-Century Japanese Puppet Theater, tr., annotated, and with introduction by Stanleigh H. Jones, Jr. 1993

The Lotus Sutra, tr. Burton Watson. Also in paperback ed. 1993

The Classic of Changes: A New Translation of the I Ching as Interpreted by Wang Bi, tr. Richard John Lynn 1994

Beyond Spring: Tz'u Poems of the Sung Dynasty, tr. Julie Landau 1994

The Columbia Anthology of Traditional Chinese Literature, ed. Victor H. Mair 1994

Scenes for Mandarins: The Elite Theater of the Ming, tr. Cyril Birch 1995

Letters of Nichiren, ed. Philip B. Yampolsky; tr. Burton Watson et al. 1996

Unforgotten Dreams: Poems by the Zen Monk Shōtetsu, tr. Steven D. Carter 1997

The Vimalakirti Sutra, tr. Burton Watson 1997

Japanese and Chinese Poems to Sing: The Wakan rōei shū, tr. J. Thomas Rimer and Jonathan Chaves 1997

Breeze Through Bamboo: Kanshi of Ema Saikō, tr. Hiroaki Sato 1998

A Tower for the Summer Heat, by Li Yu, tr. Patrick Hanan 1998

Traditional Japanese Theater: An Anthology of Plays, by Karen Brazell 1998

The Original Analects: Sayings of Confucius and His Successors (0479–0249), by E. Bruce Brooks and A. Taeko Brooks 1998

The Classic of the Way and Virtue: A New Translation of the Tao-te ching of Laozi as Interpreted by Wang Bi, tr. Richard John Lynn 1999

The Four Hundred Songs of War and Wisdom: An Anthology of Poems from Classical Tamil, The Puṟanāṉūṟu, ed. and tr. George L. Hart and Hank Heifetz 1999

Original Tao: Inward Training (Nei-yeh) and the Foundations of Taoist Mysticism, by Harold D. Roth 1999

Po Chü-i: Selected Poems, tr. Burton Watson 2000

Lao Tzu's Tao Te Ching: A Translation of the Startling New Documents Found at Guodian, by Robert G. Henricks 2000

The Shorter Columbia Anthology of Traditional Chinese Literature, ed. Victor H. Mair 2000

Mistress and Maid (Jiaohongji), by Meng Chengshun, tr. Cyril Birch 2001

Chikamatsu: Five Late Plays, tr. and ed. C. Andrew Gerstle 2001

The Essential Lotus: Selections from the Lotus Sutra, tr. Burton Watson 2002

Early Modern Japanese Literature: An Anthology, 1600–1900, ed. Haruo Shirane 2002; abridged 2008

The Columbia Anthology of Traditional Korean Poetry, ed. Peter H. Lee 2002

The Sound of the Kiss, or The Story That Must Never Be Told: Pingali Suranna's Kalapurnodayamu, tr. Vecheru Narayana Rao and David Shulman 2003

The Selected Poems of Du Fu, tr. Burton Watson 2003

Far Beyond the Field: Haiku by Japanese Women, tr. Makoto Ueda 2003

Just Living: Poems and Prose by the Japanese Monk Tonna, ed. and tr. Steven D. Carter 2003

Han Feizi: Basic Writings, tr. Burton Watson 2003

Mozi: Basic Writings, tr. Burton Watson 2003

Xunzi: Basic Writings, tr. Burton Watson 2003

Zhuangzi: Basic Writings, tr. Burton Watson 2003

The Awakening of Faith, Attributed to Aśvaghosha, tr. Yoshito S. Hakeda, introduction by Ryuichi Abe 2005